The Verge of Philosophy

The Verge of Philosophy

JOHN SALLIS

The University of Chicago Press ❋ Chicago and London

JOHN SALLIS is the Frederick J. Adelmann Professor of Philosophy at Boston College and a regular visiting professor at the Universität Freiburg. He is the author of many books, including, most recently, *Topographies, Platonic Legacies, On Translation, Force of Imagination, Chorology*, and *Shades—Of Painting at the Limit*.

The University of Chicago Press, Chicago 60637
The University of Chicago Press, Ltd., London
© 2008 by The University of Chicago
All rights reserved. Published 2008
Printed in the United States of America
17 16 15 14 13 12 11 10 09 08   1 2 3 4 5
ISBN-13: 978-0-226-73430-9 (cloth)
ISBN-10: 0-226-73430-7 (cloth)

Library of Congress Cataloging-in-Publication Data

Sallis, John, 1938–
    The verge of philosophy / John Sallis.
        p. cm.
    Includes bibliographical references and index.
    ISBN-13: 978-0-226-73430-9 (cloth : alk. paper)
    ISBN-10: 0-226-73430-7 (cloth : alk. paper)
    1. Philosophy.   2. Plato.   I. Title.
    B53.S237   2008
    190—dc22
                                        2007014183

In memory of Jacques Derrida

"...nous sommes aujourd'hui à la veille de Platonisme."

«JACQUES DERRIDA, *"La Pharmacie de Platon"*»

Contents

Acknowledgments

I am grateful for permission to use material that appeared in *Heidegger and the Greeks*, edited by Drew Hyland and John Manoussakis (Bloomington and Indianapolis: Indiana University Press, 2006), pages 177–90; and material from my article "Last Words: Generosity and Reserve," which appeared in *Mosaic, a journal for the interdisciplinary study of literature*, vol. 39. 3 (September 2006), pages 15–26. Thanks also to Nancy Fedrow and Shane Ewegen for their generous assistance.

Boston
March 2007

Exordium

Near the beginning of *Richard the Second*, Bolingbroke denounces Mowbray, charging him, in his presence, with treason and murder. Bolingbroke pledges to King Richard that what he says about Mowbray he will prove on the field of battle:

> Besides, I say, and will in battle prove,
> Or here, or elsewhere to the furthest verge
> That ever was surveyed by English eye,
> That all the treasons for these eighteen years
> Complotted and contrivèd in this land
> Fetch from false Mowbray, their first head and spring.[1]

The extent of the field is a measure of Bolingbroke's resolve. Both are almost unlimited. In the end, his resolve will prove such that he will succeed in deposing the corrupt king, his deed redounding to the benefit of all of England. Yet, from the start, the extent

---

1. William Shakespeare, *The Tragedy of King Richard the Second* (I.i.92–97), in *The Complete Signet Classic Shakespeare*, ed. Sylvan Barnet (New York: Harcourt Brace Jovanovich, 1979). A verge need not as such be remote. It may be as almost unlimitedly close as the farthest verge is distant. Thus, later in the play Gaunt says to Richard: "A thousand flatterers sit within thy crown, / Whose compass is no bigger than thy head, / And yet incagèd in so small a verge / The waste is no whit lesser than thy land" (II.i.100–103).

of his resolve will have been indicated by that of a field limited only by the broadest horizon, by

> . . . the furthest verge
> That ever was surveyed by English eye,

by the outermost boundary, by the most extreme bound known to his people. Yet, however extensive the field may be, even if—as he says—it is bounded only by the furthest verge, still it has a limit, one that is defined politically, by reference to a people, by reference to what

> . . . ever was surveyed by English eye[.]

The limit is supposed to be definite, even if remote; yet it is not a limit that could be definitely fixed, that could be determined. Nonetheless it delimits also a beyond, providing a definite (yet indeterminable) limit delimiting the field of all that lies outside this furthest verge. Though definite with regard to its limit, this other field, never surveyed by English eye, is, from the operative perspective, more indefinite, precisely because it has never been surveyed by English eye. The verge itself is both the most definite and the least definite. On the one hand, it is the very source of definiteness; it defines the areas this side of and beyond the furthest verge and thereby bestows on each its definiteness. On the other hand, the verge not only is indeterminable but also is duplicitous in its relation to the two areas it delimits, belonging both to each and to neither. The verge lies neither on the side of what

> . . . ever was surveyed by English eye,

nor on the side that English eye has never seen. Yet, in a sense, it belongs to both fields, forms the edge of each, like the verges—as they are called—of green turf that gardeners use to separate their flower beds from the gravel walks that run through the garden. Belonging to both, the verge belongs also to neither, retreating, as it were, to a middle ground that is less ground than abyss. For whether the verge itself has ever been surveyed by English eye remains undecidable.

All originary determination is situated on the verge. All determination in and through which something is brought about that is entirely unprecedented takes place on the verge. This is most purely the case when what is brought about is also itself originary in the sense of taking up an orientation to origins that would not have been manifest prior to this determination. Because philosophy would be the most radical such orientation, it must to the highest degree submit to the verge; it must assent to being itself determined as such on the verge. The place at which philosophy comes to be established as such, the place from which it comes to be determined as such, is neither simply outside philosophy nor simply within it. The authority of founding belongs to the verge; in this respect it is significant that the oldest sense of the word (from which there is a semantic flow to the more recent senses) is that of a rod or staff (from Latin *virga*) symbolic of an office (as, for example, carried before a church official in processions). It is also significant in this same respect that, in a very archaic usage, *verge* could designate a type of torch or candle.

If philosophy is regarded in terms of the dynamics of its unfolding, then its founding can legitimately be traced back to Plato. This is especially the case if, with Heidegger, the course of philosophy is taken to be coextensive with the epoch in which the fundamental governing distinction (governing even the sense of fundamental) is that between the intelligible and the sensible. For it is primarily through Plato, in texts such as the *Republic*, that this distinction, which provides the most originary articulation of being as such and as a whole, comes to be established and, in being established, serves to determine philosophy as such. Even if there exists greater solidarity between Plato and his predecessors than would seem thus to be granted, even if—as has been demonstrated—there is much in the dialogues that contests and limits the otherwise exclusive operation of this distinction at the fundamental level, these displacements can be effected only if the fundamental governance of the distinction is first granted and allowed to unfold toward its limit.

The determination of philosophy as such is addressed at several points in the *Republic* but nowhere more thoroughly and persistently than in Book 7. Indeed, one could say that in Book 7 this is almost the sole concern: in telling the story of the cave, Socrates, at the outset, broaches this determination, and then, throughout the remainder of Book 7, reiterates it in various connections and directions. Among these reiterations, these repetitions of the determination of philosophy, the most extensive is that in which Socrates lays out the course of studies by which one would be brought to philosophy. The particular determination that is perhaps most explicit of all is set forth by way of introducing the curricular exposition. The question posed is that of how the would-be philosophers will be led up to the light, as if ascending from Hades. Socrates answers: "Then, as it seems, this would not be the twirling of a shell but the turning around of the soul from a nocturnal day to the true day, the ascent to being, which we shall truly affirm to be philosophy."[2]

The passage draws a contrast, setting out the determination of philosophy through the contrast with the twirling of a shell. The reference is to the game of ὀστρακίνδα. In this game, the players were divided into two groups, separated by a line. A shell (or sometimes a potsherd), black on one side and white on the other, was spun around on the ground by one of the players, who at the same time shouted νὺξ ἢ ἡμέρα (night or day—that is, the black side or the white side). Depending on whether the black side or the white side fell facing up, one group ran away and the other went in pursuit.[3] It seems clear from the passage that Socrates' primary intent is to contrast the twirling that initiates this

---

2. *Rep.* 521c. Further references to Platonic dialogues are given in the text. Translations of Platonic texts are my own, though I have consulted existing translations.

3. See James Adam, *The Republic of Plato*, 2 vols. (Cambridge: Cambridge University Press, 1965), 2:105, 181–83. This game is also mentioned by Socrates in the course of his first speech in the *Phaedrus*. Describing the lover whose love has ceased, Socrates says that he will not keep the pledges made to his former beloved but will evade them, run

game with the turning that will be identified as constituting philosophy; the crux of the contrast is presumably that philosophy is not an affair of no consequence, dependent largely on chance. On the other hand, one might well wonder whether the mere juxtaposition might, despite the contrast, allude to the affinity between philosophy and play that is more openly displayed by certain other passages in the *Republic*.[4]

In any event, this particular game is akin to philosophy inasmuch as both involve turning something around: in the one case the shell, in the other, the soul. Socrates explicitly describes philosophy as a turning around (περιαγωγή), resuming the designation put in play in the very first reiteration of the story of the cave. In particular, philosophy involves a turning around from one kind of day to another, from a nocturnal day, a day that is like night, to the true day—just as in the twirling of the shell, the alternation is between black and white and the outcome is "night or day." Nocturnal day, a kind of day in which all things would be shrouded in darkness, is suggestive of the condition that prevails within the cave, while true day, one in which all things would lie unconcealed before our eyes, is suggestive of the condition that prevails for the prisoner who has escaped to the open expanse outside the cave. The passage thus reiterates the story of the escape from the cave and then, appropriately, concludes with the explicit determination of philosophy as the ascent to being.[5] Socrates declares—in a deferred performative—that this will be truly affirmed to be philosophy; that is, that this affirmation will prove to be such as to disclose philosophy unconcealedly. This affirmation,

---

away from them: "The shell has fallen with the other side up; and he changes his part and runs away; and the other is compelled to pursue him" (*Phaedr.* 241b).

4. Most significant in this regard is the comedy of the πόλις, which occupies much of Book 5. See my discussion in *Being and Logos: Reading the Platonic Dialogues*, 3rd ed. (Bloomington: Indiana University Press, 1996), 371–78.

5. The word ἐπάνοδος can mean *return* as well as *ascent*, in contrast to the word ἀνάβασις, which Plato uses elsewhere in Book 7 and which means only *ascent*. The double meaning of ἐπάνοδος, suggesting that the ascent to being is a return of the soul to being, invokes a mythical background that resembles that of the *Phaedrus* more than that of the *Republic*.

marking these two figures (the turning around of the soul and the ascent to being) precisely *as* constituting the determination of philosophy, is what makes this passage exceptional among the various reiterations ventured in Book 7.

This determination of philosophy does not lie simply outside philosophy. The very terms in which it is formulated—most notably, as the ascent to being—require certain rigorous operations that are barely conceivable apart from philosophy. And yet, the reference to the game of twirling the shell, intensified by the common reference to night and day, hints that what lies outside is not entirely irrelevant to the determination of philosophy. Still more decisive is Socrates' refusal—following the exposition of the curriculum—to proceed, as Glaucon requests, to the highest— the truly philosophical—level that both the figure of the divided line and the story of the cave serve to project (see *Rep.* 532d–33a). Even erotic Glaucon—and ἔρως belongs inseparably to the performative determination, just as an archaic reference to it belongs among the manifold senses of *verge*[6]—must learn to hold back. The determination of philosophy as ascent to being, that is, as ascent from sensible to intelligible, does not yet fully effect the ascent; it falls short of philosophy itself. It remains—and, as a determination *of* philosophy, must remain—on the verge of philosophy.

Philosophy can thus be said to begin on the verge, provided beginning is understood as originary determination.

The same can be said of the end, that it too takes place on the verge of philosophy, provided the reference is to the enactment of the inversion and displacement of the distinction set out in the beginning. This enactment no longer simply belongs to philosophy, no longer resumes the fundamental distinction by which philosophy was originarily determined; and yet, it can in no wise dispense with the conceptual and linguistic resources of philosophy but must employ these in setting out the dissolution of

6. In a very old, long since obsolete sense, retained afterwards in zoology, *verge* designates the male reproductive organ of a mollusk, crustacean, or other invertebrate.

philosophy. No longer claimed by the first beginning, it has nonetheless at its disposal nothing but the means stemming from this beginning, for it has not yet crossed over to another beginning. On the other hand, it cannot but be drawn in this direction, even if without yet seeing the opening toward which it moves. Enacting the end of philosophy is, at once, engaging its mutation, while sensing also the threat posed by mutation into sheer nonphilosophy, the threat of a loss of self, of the loss of that which first stirred as the beginning of philosophy was prepared.

The enactment thus belongs both within and beyond philosophy and yet neither within nor beyond. This duplicity of the verge is so deeply inscribed that it threatens to split the verge, to divide the limit from itself. This is why Derrida outlines two strategies, two motifs of deconstruction, that—as he says—a new writing must weave and interlace. One strategy is, in his words, to use "against the edifice the instruments or stones available in the house, that is, equally, in the language."[7] Derrida suggests that this is the style characteristic of the Heideggerian questions (his mention of the house clearly refers to Heidegger's celebrated metaphor); yet he grants that there are exceptions, that "there are also breaks and changes of terrain in texts of the Heideggerian type." To this extent these texts also border on the second strategy, that of changing terrain, "in a discontinuous and irruptive fashion, by brutally placing oneself outside and by affirming an absolute break and difference." Though Derrida takes this motif to be the one dominant in France at the time (the text, "The Ends of Man," is dated May 12, 1968), his subsequent reference to "the increasingly insistent and increasingly rigorous recourse to Nietzsche in France" has the effect of introducing a mutation of the twofold motif into that of a difference between two eves: one eve is "the guard mounted around the house"; the other is "the awakening to the day that is coming." Yet *veille* means *eve*

---

7. Jacques Derrida, *Marges de la philosophie* (Paris: Les Éditions de Minuit, 1972), 162. Translated by Alan Bass as *Margins of Philosophy* (Chicago: University of Chicago Press, 1982), 135. This as well as the subsequent citations are taken from the concluding section of the text "Les Fins de l'homme" ("The Ends of Man").

not only in the sense of a period of time (evening) but also in the sense of a time in which one keeps vigil, a time of watchfulness in which there is also a directedness to the day to come (as in the English phrase: on the eve of battle). The word thus has the figurative senses of *point, brink,* and indeed *verge.* Derrida's proposal that "we are perhaps between these two *veilles*" can hence be understood as placing us between two verges, associated on the one side with Heidegger ("the guard mounted around the house") and on the other side with Nietzsche ("the awakening to the day that is coming"). To be between these verges means to think in the duplicity of the verge on which we are set in the end of philosophy. The imperative placed upon such thinking is to weave together, to interlace, the two sides, to repair the split while remaining also within its tension, accommodating thinking to the complex figure of the verge.

Or rather, this would have been the imperative at that time, in 1968. If, at that time, Derrida's final question, "But who, we?", expressed most succinctly the way in which "The Ends of Man" put in question the phenomenological *we,* disrupting its unity with natural consciousness, installing us instead between two *veilles,* today the question reaches still further. For in our very different time, it must be asked: do we today, we of today, stand under the same imperative? Is it still incumbent upon us to think the verge, to think on the verge, in accord with the figure drawn in Derrida's 1968 text?

There can be no question but that the verge has undergone mutation, that its shape has changed on both of the edges into which it threatens to split. For unprecedented kinds of openings have taken shape, openings both back toward the first beginning and beyond toward another beginning. Even the primacy accorded the question, as signaled by the placement of the question of the *we* as the conclusion of Derrida's 1968 text, has, meanwhile, given way to the question of the question.

For thinking on the verge, for the self-figuration of thinking as on the verge, the openings back toward the first beginning are especially pertinent. For, in the Platonic beginning in which philosophy is originally determined, thinking is, as we have seen, also—yet in a different way—on the verge. In taking up the opening toward this beginning, thinking is stretched, as it were, between two verges, stationing itself at one in such a way as to move back to engagement with the other. Such a figure is intimated—though still from a distance—in Derrida's first study of Plato, the essay, "Plato's Pharmacy," published in 1972. Here again it is of a *veille* that Derrida writes: "we are today on the *veille* of Platonism"[8]—on the eve on which we stay awake, keep vigil, remain watchful for the Platonism that is to come with the dawn. We are on the verge of Platonism, on the verge of a new engagement with the verge of philosophy, the verge on which its originary determination was carried out. Derrida adds that this eve/verge of Platonism "can also, naturally, be thought as the day after [*lendemain*] Hegelianism." The day after Hegelianism denotes in shorthand the verge in the end of philosophy;[9] and it

8. Derrida, "La Pharmacie de Platon," in *La Dissémination* (Paris: Éditions du Seuil, 1972), 122f. Translated by Barbara Johnson as *Dissemination* (Chicago: University of Chicago Press, 1981), 107. Further references to this work will be indicated in the text by *D*, followed by the page numbers in the French and the English editions, respectively.

9. Derrida marks in various ways the manifoldness and complexity of this verge, considered specifically in relation to Hegel's thought. For example, in *Of Grammatology* he characterizes Hegel as "the last philosopher of the book and the first thinker of writing" (*De la Grammatologie* [Paris: Les Éditions de Minuit, 1967], 41. Translated by Gayatri Spivak as *Of Grammatology* [Baltimore: The Johns Hopkins University Press, 1974], 26). In an interview that took place in 1971, Derrida remarks that in his lecture "La différance" (1968) everything is played out "at a point of almost absolute proximity to Hegel" (*Positions* [Paris: Les Éditions de Minuit, 1972], 60. Translated by Alan Bass as *Positions* [Chicago: University of Chicago Press, 1981], 44; hereafter citations refer to French/English pagination). In the same interview he says, marking the complexity and tension: "If there were a definition of *différance*, it would be precisely the limit, the interruption, the destruction of the Hegelian *relève* [Derrida's translation of *Aufhebung*] wherever it operates" (*Positions* 55/40f.). He adds that elucidating the relation to Hegel would be "difficult labor ... which in a certain way is interminable, at least if one wishes to execute it rigorously and minutely" (*Positions* 59/43f.). Much later in the same interview he says: "We will never be finished with the reading or rereading of the Hegelian text, and, in a certain way, I do nothing other than attempt to explain myself on this point. In effect I believe that Hegel's text is necessarily fissured; that it is something more and other than the circular closure of its representation" (*Positions* 103/77).

is as situated on this verge that we come to be on the verge of Platonism. Yet the move is no mere return: coming to be on the verge of Platonism is, at once, to engage also the movement beyond to another beginning, to the dawn on the morn after Hegelianism. Still, it is to do so in a way that reawakens much that belonged to Platonism in its beginning: its choric cosmology, its ear for music, its proximity to the question of politics.

On the verge of philosophy nothing becomes more difficult, more problematic, than discourse itself, not only as such but also in the particular guise it assumes at this limit. As thinking ventures to hover between the verges of beginning and end, its discourse inevitably doubles up and recoils upon itself, undoing what it says in the very saying of it. For on the verge discourse loses the security granted it by philosophy, the security provided by the precedence of intelligibility. Another writing, another comportment to discourse, is imperative.

As already in this exordium. For, even if another name marks here a certain reservation and retreat, prefacing—which, as we have known since Hegel, is, strictly speaking, impossible—has in the present instance been deployed; and it has sought to station itself on the verge and to begin responding to the imperative of another writing and thinking.

1

Plato's Other Beginning

Beginning is what is most formidable.

Think of the beginning of a sentence or of an essay or of an entire book. The beginning, the very first word, must anticipate, before anything has been said, all that will be said. With the first word, the whole of what one would say must already be in play, even if one's intention never simply precedes its realization in speech, even if one genuinely knows what one wants to say only when one has succeeded in saying it. Or think of the beginning of an intricate geometrical proof, of how the first equation or construction must anticipate, before it has been traversed, the entire course of the proof. In order to begin, one must somehow know what, on the other hand, one cannot, as one begins, yet know. Or imagine a painter at the moment when he first puts brush to canvas. At that moment when he begins to paint, the entire picture must somehow be in view, even though as such it cannot be in view, not even, as we say, in the mind's eye. Imagine—or, though the prospect is daunting, at least *try* to imagine—a composer as he sets down the very first note or chord, hearing somehow at that moment the entire, still unsounded composition, the composition that even when sounded will necessarily be sounded and heard, not in a moment, but across an expanse of time. Could one ever hope to imagine how Beethoven, almost totally deaf, could have sensed where to begin so as to arrive, with artistic necessity, at the choral setting of *An die Freude?*

And yet—if bordering on the unimaginable—beginnings are made. Sometimes their character as beginnings is emphasized, as when one begins with a discourse about beginning. Or as in the final movement of the *Ninth Symphony,* which begins by quoting, in order, the themes of the preceding movements, interrupting each, in turn, before then letting the final theme begin to sound very softly in the double-basses, as if emerging from silent depths.

Even as a beginning is made—and one hardly knows how—it remains formidable. For one cannot but be keenly aware from the beginning, in the very moment when one begins, that the stakes are very high indeed. If the beginning is faulty or limited, everything will be compromised. Eventually one will be compelled to return to the beginning, to make another beginning that compensates for what was lacking in the first beginning. Or rather, to make another beginning that *attempts insofar as possible* to compensate: for one cannot always simply undo having already begun.

In the Platonic dialogues, too, beginning is nothing less than formidable. As interrogated and as enacted, beginnings are pervasive in the dialogues. For instance, the ascent represented and enacted at the center of the *Republic* is described as an ascent to the beginning of the whole (ἐπὶ τὴν τοῦ παντὸς ἀρχήν) (*Rep.* 511b–c). It is also, at once, an ascent from the cave-like condition in which humans find themselves in the beginning—hence an ascent from one beginning to another, from—as Aristotle will put it—what is first for us to what is first in itself. Furthermore, one could think of the question of the city,[1] the question that overarches the entire dialogue, as a question of beginning, as a question of how to begin anew with a city as secure as possible from the corruption to which political life is otherwise exposed.

---

1. The word πόλις has been translated throughout as *city.* This translation, which follows current practice, should not however obscure the difference between the Greek πόλις and the modern city (and state). See the discussion of the sense of the Greek πόλις in Martin Heidegger's *Parmenides,* vol. 54 of *Gesamtausgabe* (Frankfurt A.M.: Vittorio Klostermann, 1982), 130–44.

This aspect of the political question reaches its comedic climax when it turns out that the founding of such a city will require the expulsion of all who are more than ten years old. In order to begin anew, it must become a city of children (see *Rep.* 541a).

The *Timaeus* is even more permeated with the enactment and interrogation of beginnings. Indeed an injunction as to how to begin is set forth in the dialogue: "With regard to everything it is most important to begin at the natural beginning" (*Tim.* 29b). And yet—most remarkably—the *Timaeus* itself violates the very injunction it sets forth. Not only does it defer the beginning of Timaeus' speech, inserting prior to it speeches by Socrates and Critias that are quite different in character; but also, even once Timaeus begins to speak, it turns out that he has not begun at the natural beginning and so is eventually compelled by the very drift of the discourse to interrupt his discourse and set out on another, to make another beginning.

Even if this other beginning in the *Timaeus* has a certain distinctiveness, even if its sense is incomparable, it is not as such unique. Indeed the dialogues abound with various kinds of fresh starts and new beginnings. One of the most decisive occurs in the dialogue in which all the discursive and dramatic elements are brought to utmost concentration on the end, on death; precisely here, in the *Phaedo,* as the centralmost discourse of this dialogue, there is an account of Socrates' beginning, of his venturing another beginning. As he prepares to die, Socrates turns to the past, to his own beginning; he tells his friends the story of how he first began with a kind of direct investigation of nature and of how, after such investigations failed, he came to set out on a second sailing by turning from things to λόγοι, making thus another beginning. But among all the polyphonic discourses of the Platonic dialogues, there are none in which this turn to λόγοι has not already been taken. It is always the second sailing that bears Platonic thought along. It is as though Platonic thought makes its first beginning only in launching another beginning, as if, in first beginning, it already sets out on another beginning.

>>><<<

It cannot but appear remarkable, then, that Heidegger writes of the first beginning in terms that, though generalized, more or less identify this beginning with Plato. At the very least it will be necessary to say, in response, that if indeed Plato's thought constitutes a first beginning, it will prove to be a far more complex beginning than the expression *first beginning* might at first suggest. For within this alleged first beginning there are, as the examples just cited show, multiple instances of another beginning.

Yet a great deal more specificity is required in order, first of all, to determine the precise sense in which Heidegger takes Platonic thought to be the first beginning and then, secondly, to hear the resonance evoked in the Platonic texts themselves by this characterization. In listening to this resonance, it will be a matter of determining whether these texts accord with and confirm the characterization of Plato's thought as first beginning or whether within these texts there are retreats that go unsounded and that can effectively recoil on that characterization.

What, then, does Heidegger mean by first beginning? In *Contributions to Philosophy* this expression designates the beginning of philosophy, of what later comes to be called metaphysics. The first beginning occurs in and through the Platonic determination of being as ἰδέα. This determination establishes the distinction between intelligible ἰδέα and sensible thing as the fundamental— that is, the founding—distinction of philosophy or metaphysics. This distinction provides then the fundamental framework for all subsequent philosophy or metaphysics. The sequence of determinations of and within this framework constitutes the history of metaphysics, which reaches its end when, in Nietzsche's thought, the distinction between intelligible and sensible is completely inverted and thus its possibilities finally exhausted.

In designating this beginning as the *first* beginning, Heidegger does not intend to suggest that it is a *simple* beginning. It is not a matter of a beginning made for the first time, preceded by nothing else of its kind. Indeed it turns out that what Heidegger takes to occur in Plato's thought is a beginning *in the form* of a transformation, a redetermination, a change. As founding metaphysics, this beginning is *first* only in distinction from the other beginning that would be ventured beyond the end of metaphysics. This other beginning is what *Contributions to Philosophy* would prepare—that is, this text is engaged in crossing over to the other beginning.

How are the two beginnings related? There are expressions in other texts, if not in *Contributions* itself, that suggest a certain mutual externality, such expressions as *Überwindung*—or even *Verwindung—der Metaphysik*. The relation would, then, be such that what was begun in the first beginning would have run its course, have come to its end, so that now this first beginning could be left behind—as something overcome, gotten over—as one ventures another beginning. And yet, there is no such externality: in venturing another beginning, one does not simply leave the first beginning behind; one does not simply abandon the metaphysics to which the first beginning gave rise. In *Contributions to Philosophy* Heidegger writes: "The other beginning is the more originary taking-over of the concealed essence of philosophy."[2] Thus, in the other beginning something essential to philosophy that, on the other hand, remained concealed from philosophy is to be taken over in a way that is more originary than was the case in philosophy. It is to be taken over in such a way that it does not remain, as in philosophy, simply concealed.

Thus the other beginning, beginning beyond the end of metaphysics, is at the same time a return to the first beginning, a return that enters into the first beginning so as to grasp it more originarily than in the first beginning, so as to grasp somehow that which, though essential to the first beginning, remained—in the first beginning—concealed. The double character of this move, that it is a move beyond metaphysics that, at once, goes back into the beginning, is perhaps most succinctly expressed in the following passage from *Contributions to Philosophy*: "The leap into the other

2. Martin Heidegger, *Beiträge zur Philosophie (Vom Ereignis)*, vol. 65 of *Gesamtausgabe* (Frankfurt A.M.: Vittorio Klostermann, 1989), §259. Translations are my own. Further references to this work will be indicated in the text by *BP*, followed by section number.

beginning is a return into the first beginning, and vice versa. . . . The return into the first beginning is . . . precisely a distancing from it, a taking up of that distance-positioning [*Fernstellung*] that is necessary in order to experience what began in and as that beginning. For *without* this distance-positioning—and only a positioning in the other beginning is a sufficient one—we remain always, in an entangling way, too close to the beginning, insofar as we are roofed over and covered [*überdacht und zugedeckt*] by what issues from the beginning" (*BP* §91). One could say: what is decisive is to move through the first beginning, to move disclosively from the first beginning back to that which, though essential to it, remained, in the first beginning, concealed. What is decisive is the move from the intelligible-sensible framework that governed metaphysics back to what within that framework remained concealed. What is decisive is the move from the Platonic determination of being as ἰδέα back to that which, precisely through this determination, came to be concealed.

Heidegger insists on the distance required in order to carry out this move. He insists that sufficient distance is provided only by being positioned in the other beginning, that is, only from a stance beyond metaphysics, only from the position that results from twisting free of the Platonic-metaphysical distinction between intelligible and sensible. Only if one gets out from under the roof of metaphysics can one—according to Heidegger—find one's way back from the determination of being as ἰδέα, back to that which came to be concealed precisely through this determination. Heidegger is insistent: only from the distance of the other beginning can one carry out this regress within—this regress back through—the first beginning.

It is this insistence that I want to put in question. My intent, however, is not to show that such a regress is broached at certain critical junctures in the history of metaphysics, though there are indeed crucial indications of this in, for instance, Plotinus, Schelling, and Nietzsche. Leaving open in the present context the question whether such a regress remains closed to those who remain under the roof of metaphysics, the question I want to raise concerns Plato himself. Can one mark in the Platonic texts themselves a regress from the determination of being as ἰδέα to that which subsequently in the history of metaphysics remains essentially concealed? Does Plato in founding metaphysics also destabilize it through a regression to that which escapes metaphysics? Does there belong to the first beginning a countermovement toward another beginning, Plato's other beginning?

In order to develop this question, it is necessary to focus on the interpretation of Plato that is at work in Heidegger's determination of Platonic thought as constituting the first beginning. This interpretation is primarily that expressed in *Plato's Doctrine of Truth,* the redaction of which belongs to the very years in which Heidegger composed *Contributions to Philosophy* and the other manuscripts closely linked to it. If one takes *Contributions to Philosophy* as carrying out primarily the leap into another beginning, one can regard *Plato's Doctrine of Truth* as carrying out the complementary return into the first beginning.

Since *Plato's Doctrine of Truth* seems to go furthest in this complementary direction, I shall limit my discussion to it.[3] Although this text is well known—perhaps all too well known—I will need to crystallize the parameters and the determining schema of the interpretation developed in this text. In this way it will be possible to mark with some precision the limit of Heidegger's interpretation of Plato's thought as first beginning and also to draw from Heidegger's texts certain resources for rethinking what Heidegger puts in question, for rethinking this questionable moment

3. There are two lecture-courses that cover much the same material as *Plato's Doctrine of Truth* and that clearly provided the basis for Heidegger's redaction of the essay. The first constitutes the initial half of the course *Vom Wesen der Wahrheit* presented in the Winter Semester 1931–32 (published as vol. 34 of *Gesamtausgabe* [Frankfurt A.M.: Vittorio Klostermann, 1988]). The second constitutes the initial half of the course of the same title presented in the Winter Semester 1933–34 (published in *Sein und Wahrheit*, vol. 36–37 of *Gesamtausgabe* [Frankfurt A.M.: Vittorio Klostermann, 2001]). In both cases the second half of the course consisted in interpretation of selected passages from the *Theaetetus*.

beyond the debate with this text. Yet even as we retrace the configuration of Heidegger's text, some features may begin to strike
us as strange, if not as outright provocative.

Radicalizing and ironizing an ancient distinction, Heidegger casts his interpretation as one directed to Plato's teaching
(*Lehre*) regarding truth, as aiming to say what remains unsaid
in the Platonic text. At the very outset—most remarkably—he
says this unsaid, exposes in writing the unwritten teaching, thus
already in the beginning circling back from the interpretation,
still to come, that will uncover the hidden teaching. It is as if the
text—this text on beginnings—began by transposing the end,
the outcome of the interpretation, to the beginning. Even before
the text to be interpreted is cited, Heidegger says what only the
interpretation of that text can reveal, says the unsaid, writes the
unwritten: "What remains unsaid there [that is, in the text still to
be cited, translated, and interpreted] is a change [*eine Wendung*]
in the determination of the essence of truth."[4] From this beginning one can read off, in advance, most of the parameters as well
as the determining schema of the ensuing interpretation. Two
determinations of truth will be exhibited: first, the Preplatonic
determination and, then, the determination that is effected in the
Platonic text and that comes to prevail in the history of metaphysics. It is to be shown that in the Platonic text—specifically in
the passage with which Book 7 of the *Republic* begins—a change
is effected from the earlier determination to what will become
the metaphysical determination. It will turn out that what effects
this change, what drives the transition from one determination
of truth to the other, is the Platonic determination of being as
ἰδέα.

The schema can also be construed from the perspective of *Contributions to Philosophy.* Then, over against the exhibiting of the
constitution of the first beginning, there would take shape a double gesture with respect to the older determination of truth: on

4. Heidegger, *Platons Lehre von der Wahrheit,* in *Wegmarken,* vol. 9 of *Gesamtausgabe* (Frankfurt A.M.: Vittorio Klostermann, 1976), 203. Further references are given in the text as *GA* 9 followed by page numbers.

the one hand, the regression that recovers it by moving through the first beginning; on the other hand, a demonstration of how in Plato's text a repression of this other determination is already operative.

Turning to the beginning of Book 7 of the *Republic*, where Socrates enjoins Glaucon to "make an image of our nature in its education and lack of education," Heidegger proceeds to interpret the passage that ensues, letting the interpretation be discreetly guided by the most telling words in Plato's text. One such word is παιδεία, rendered as *Bildung* or, with reservations, as *education*. The image that Socrates makes for Glaucon, that he describes and asks Glaucon to envision, has to do with education. By casting what he says in relation to the image of a cave, Socrates makes an image of our nature in its education and lack of education. Thus the image that Socrates actually makes and Glaucon envisions is not just that of a cave but rather of the movement through which the soul undergoes education. The expression by which Socrates describes this movement is περιαγωγὴ ὅλης τῆς ψυχῆς, a revolution or turning-around of the entire soul. Heidegger emphasizes this turning-around; and in order to designate that to which this turning-around is oriented, he brings into play another of the telling words used by Socrates in the passage. It is for Heidegger the most telling word: τὸ ἀληθές, which Heidegger translates, not as *das Wahre* (*the true*), but as *das Unverborgene* (*the unconcealed*). In this translation, in the shift that it effects, Heidegger's entire interpretation is broached.

The image of our nature that Socrates makes is thus an image of the way of education as a way on which the soul turns around toward the unconcealed. What the image actually lays out, according to Heidegger, are the four stages belonging to this way. Turning away from the captivating images within the cave, the soul comes to see more unconcealedly the things of which it had previously seen only images. Proceeding still further, emerging from the cave into the open space above, the soul comes to behold the very look of things, that is, the εἴδη that shine through things and make them look as they do. It comes to behold the εἴδη themselves and no longer merely the εἴδη shining from afar through things. Here there is genuine liberation as the soul comes before the most unconcealed (τὸ ἀληθέστατον). And yet, the progression through these three stages, this progression toward the ever more unconcealed, requires still another, a fourth, stage. Only if the image is extended to include finally a return to the cave does it genuinely image our nature in its education *and lack* of education. It is the privation that prescribes the final stage: because lack of education (ἀπαιδευσία), that is, ignorance, is never simply left behind, education requires continual engagement with and overcoming of this condition. For Heidegger this stage, too, is determined by orientation to unconcealment. The unconcealed must, he says, always be wrested from concealment, and so to unconcealment as such there belongs a continual overcoming of concealment. Παιδεία reaches its fulfillment only in a modality of unconcealment in which this essential connection to concealment is appropriated. In returning to the cave, the escaped prisoner enacts such an appropriation.

These brief indications suffice to show how Heidegger's interpretation begins. His first move is to show how the originary Greek determination of truth as unconcealment remains operative in this Socratic discourse on education. Not only are the stages of education determined by orientation to unconcealment but also in the very image of a cave there is imaged the character of unconcealment: a cave is an open space in which things can appear in a certain light, an open space that is yet enclosed, just as unconcealment—which in other contexts Heidegger calls: the open space of a clearing—is, as it were, enclosed by the concealment from which it must be wrested. Thus, Heidegger's first move is to recover the older determination of truth as it is still operative in the Platonic text. Even before laying out the first beginning, Heidegger has already carried out the regression through it to the originary determination of truth as unconcealment.

Heidegger's second move goes against the first. What he proceeds to show is that in the passage on education there is also another determination of truth at work and that this determination, which will become the metaphysical determination, is already dominant. It seems—remarkably—that what most testifies to this dominance is the shape of the story, the way the story is shaped around the various sites and moments that belong to it. In a decisive passage he writes: "The illustrative power [*Veranschaulichung*] of the 'allegory of the cave' does not come from the image of the closedness of the subterranean vault and the imprisonment of people within its confines, nor does it come from the sight of the open space outside the cave. For Plato, rather, the expository power behind the images of the 'allegory' is concentrated on the role played by the fire, the fire's glow and the shadows it casts, the brightness of day, the sunlight and the sun. Everything depends on the shining forth of whatever appears and on making its visibility possible. Certainly unhiddenness is mentioned in its various stages, but it is considered simply in terms of how it makes whatever appears be accessible in its look (εἶδος)" (*GA* 9:225). Everything seems to depend on the story's being drawn more toward one side than the other, more to the side of appearances and of what makes them possible, the glow of the fire inside the cave and the sunlight that brightens the day outside. To be sure, truth as unconcealment is also portrayed, especially in the image of the enclosed openness of the cave. But in the way the story is told—or at least as Heidegger takes it to be told—this side is dominated by the emphasis accorded to the look (εἶδος, ἰδέα) and to the lighting that enables the look to shine forth.

The outcome that Heidegger takes the story to have is well known and requires only the briefest reminder. Heidegger indicates that what has come into force in the Platonic text is a shift, which, displacing ἀλήθεια as unconcealment, sets the ἰδέα, as it were, at the center. Thus, unconcealment comes to be assimilated to the ἰδέα, comes to be regarded as made possible by the ἰδέα. Coming thus under the yoke of the ἰδέα, truth comes to be redetermined in reference to the ἰδέα, as the correctness (ὀρθότης) of vision of the ἰδέα, as agreement (ὁμοίωσις) with it. And whereas truth as unconcealment counted as a trait of beings themselves,

truth as correctness belongs to human comportment toward beings.

This, then, according to Heidegger, is the unsaid of the Platonic texts, Plato's unwritten teaching: the change from the determination of truth as unconcealment of beings to truth as the correctness of human knowledge. This is what, though happening
in the text, goes unremarked, remains unsaid.

>>><<<

If one agreed that this is indeed Plato's teaching regarding truth,
then there would be little hope of discerning in the first beginning
a countermovement that might constitute another beginning.
For Heidegger's conclusions do not allow even a genuine ambiguity to remain, much less a countermovement. Rather, there
remains only a trace of the originary determination of truth, a
trace that, because of the dominance of the ἰδέα, is already des-
tined to disappear entirely.

This is how things would stand if one agreed that what Heidegger identifies as Plato's teaching is in fact such. And yet, not
all have agreed. One who did not agree is Paul Friedländer. His
criticism of *Plato's Doctrine of Truth* and his extended exchange
with Heidegger is well known and need not be retraced here
through its various phases.[5] Suffice it to say that even when
Friedländer withdrew one of his principal criticisms and granted
that the sense of ἀλήθεια as unconcealment was in play very early
among the Greeks, he still continued to insist on his other principal criticism, his rejection of what he calls Heidegger's "historical
construction," namely, the thesis that in Plato there occurred a
change from truth as unconcealment to truth as correctness.

Another who, after the debate with Friedländer, no longer
agreed with this thesis was Heidegger himself. When I spoke with
him about Plato in 1975, I was surprised at the candidness with
which he voiced his dissatisfaction with his book *Plato's Doctrine*

---

5. See my discussion in *Delimitations: Phenomenology and the End of Metaphysics*, 2nd
ed. (Bloomington: Indiana University Press, 1995), 176–80.

of Truth. The book was, he said, no longer tenable (*nicht mehr haltbar*). Yet this only reiterated what Heidegger had written in a text composed in 1964. In the text "The End of Philosophy and the Task of Thinking" he writes, "But then the assertion about an essential transformation of truth, that is, from unconcealment to correctness, is also untenable [*nicht haltbar*]."[6]

What are the consequences of this very remarkable retraction? Can the determination of Platonic thought as the first beginning remain intact, that is, somehow be reconstituted? Can the historical framework of *Contributions to Philosophy*, the opposition between the first beginning and another beginning, remain in force, or is it, on the contrary, thoroughly destabilized? More specifically, how is the relation between the two determinations of truth to be reconfigured in the Platonic text once Heidegger's thesis of a change from one to the other has been set aside? Can it be simply a matter of now granting that the Platonic text is ambiguous or two-sided, that both senses of truth are operative there? Even then, it would still be imperative to determine just how these two senses belong together in the Platonic text.

How might one today venture such a reconfiguration—beyond the debate over Heidegger's interpretation and even in a certain countermovement to that interpretation? One possibility can be opened perhaps by something that can be gleaned from Heidegger's specific statement regarding the alleged outcome of the change in the determination of truth. In this statement Heidegger says that after the change, "The ἰδέα is not a presenting foreground [*ein darstellender Vordergrund*] of ἀλήθεια but rather the ground that makes it possible" (*GA* 9: 234). The formulation suggests—or in any case can be taken to suggest—that *prior* to the change the ἰδέα *is* a presenting foreground of ἀλήθεια. But then if there is no change, if the alleged change did not occur, one might well suppose, without limitation or qualification, that the ἰδέα simply—or not so simply—is a presenting foreground of ἀλήθεια.

6. Heidegger, *Zur Sache des Denkens* (Tübingen: Max Niemeyer Verlag, 1969), 78.

The ἰδέα would be the look by which things come to be present, the look that, shining through them, presents them as the things they are, that is, *in their unconcealment*. Yet as such the ἰδέα would be only foreground, would be set against the background of concealment from which the look of things would have to be wrested and to which these looks, the things themselves, would always remain attached. Thus the ἰδέα would be nothing other than the moment of unconcealment belonging to ἀλήθεια. But then, there would be no more demanding imperative than that the ἰδέα always be thought *in relation to concealment,* that it always be thought as bound back to concealment.

Thus one would say: the look of things stands out from and remains bound to concealment, that is, is limited by concealment. Yet the difference thus installed in the first beginning is so enormous—not to say monstrous—that its consequences are virtually unlimited. Still, it can be expressed by the slightest modification: in place of saying "Being is determined as ἰδέα," one would now say "Being as determined is ἰδέα"—or perhaps a bit more clearly: "Being as determinate, but not Being as such, is ἰδέα."

The reconfiguration of the two determinations of truth can now be very simply sketched. Truth as ἀλήθεια would make possible truth as correctness by setting forth a look, a presenting foreground, to which apprehension could correspond and so be correct. Yet the look would be bound to concealment, and consequently the apprehension would be bound always to take account of the bond to concealment. Taking account of concealment could not, however, consist in apprehending it as though it were just another look. Taking account of the bond to concealment would rather consist in setting all apprehension of looks *within its limits*. In Socratic terms, it would consist in installing all learning within the horizon of a certain awareness of ignorance. But then, the very sense of truth as correctness would—as often in the dialogues—be exposed to slippage, would begin to mutate into something that would look other than the concept of truth that can, all too easily, be traced in the history of metaphysics.

And yet, this mutant truth is perhaps not entirely missing from this history, if it is thought otherwise than simply as the history of metaphysics.

But what about the beginning? Or the beginnings?

If the moment of unconcealment is thought as ἰδέα and if it is this determination that constitutes the first beginning and founds the history of metaphysics, then in thinking the bond of the ἰδέα to concealment Plato would have installed an irreducible countermovement toward *another beginning*. This other beginning, Plato's other beginning, would occur as a turn back into concealment.

There are various passages in the *Republic* and elsewhere that broach this turn back into concealment. Let me mention briefly two such passages, both from the *Republic*.

The first passage has to do with the highest ἰδέα, ἡ τοῦ ἀγαθοῦ ἰδέα. What is meant in saying that the good is the highest idea? This idea is such that its shining, its luminosity, provides the light in which all other ideas shine; it makes possible the shining of all other ideas. Thus, whenever any idea becomes manifest and is apprehended, this highest idea must have shown itself and, it seems, have been apprehended. And yet, when immediately after telling the story of the cave, Socrates reiterates the story in such a way as to relate it to the figure of the divided line, he says of the idea of the good that it is μόγις ὁρᾶσθαι, scarcely to be seen (*Rep.* 517b). Indeed, in *Plato's Doctrine of Truth* Heidegger cites and translates this passage and then in a marginal note written in his own copy of this text he says: "ἀγαθον of course ἰδέα, but no longer coming to presence [*nicht mehr anwesend*], therefore scarcely visible" (*GA* 9: 227). Yet how can there be an idea that does not come to be present—and hence visible—considering that the very sense of idea is to be a look presentable to a vision? How can it be that precisely the highest idea, the one whose luminosity all others presuppose, is itself less than fully luminous, scarcely to be seen? Is it not a matter here of installing, at what would be the very pinnacle of unconcealment, an integral bond to concealment— indeed concealment, not just as something to be appropriated *after* the highest vision (as in the return to the cave), but as something integral to the highest vision, a refusal that would haunt it as such? Is it not a matter of granting that this highest idea is such that, in its very advance toward us, it retreats? Must it not be acknowledged that, in its very moment of self-showing, the good withdraws from view?

The second passage occurs at the point in Book 7 where Socrates most explicitly sets about reiterating the story of the cave with which Book 7 begins. Yet what is said in the relevant passage must be read against the background provided in the exposition of the figure of the line given at the end of Book 6. In the earlier discussion Socrates draws a contrast between the penultimate segment, corresponding to διάνοια, and the highest segment, corresponding to ἐπιστήμη or dialectic. At the penultimate stage, the progression of vision is, as at the lower stages, by way of images, "using as images the things that were previously imitated" (*Rep.* 510b). In this dianoetic eikasia one takes as images those things previously taken as originals and one's vision proceeds through these images to their originals. It is precisely this dyadic image-original structure that, it seems, would finally be left behind at the highest level, that of dialectic. At this level all images would, it seems, be left behind for the sake of a vision of the ἀρχή, the beginning, which is not itself an image of something else.

This discussion is then resumed in the explicit reiteration in Book 7 of the story with which it begins. Once Socrates has gone through a detailed articulation of the penultimate stage, Glaucon is eager to proceed to dialectic and to go through it in the same way so as to arrive at "that place which is for one who reaches it a haven from the road, as it were, and an end of his journey" (*Rep.* 532e). The crucial passage occurs in Socrates' answer to Glaucon's request: "You will no longer be able to follow, my dear Glaucon, although there wouldn't be any lack of eagerness on my part. But you would no longer be seeing an image of what we are saying, but rather the truth itself, at least as it looks to me" (*Rep.* 533a).

Here *the truth itself* (αὐτὸ τὸ ἀληθές) means the unconcealed; it has nothing to do with correctness. Here, at the end of the journey—figured on the line, imaged by the movement up out of the cave—one would see the original truth, the true (that is, unconcealed) original, which presumably in its pure luminosity would no longer be an image of some further original. *Or rather*, it would be a matter of seeing the truth—Socrates says—*as it looks to me* (μοι φαίνεται), that is, in the appearance that it offers to me, the *image* that it offers, casts, in my direction, *and so*, in distinction from the *look itself*. Indeed Socrates continues: "Whether it is really so or not can no longer be properly insisted on. But that there is some such thing to see must be insisted on" (*Rep.* 533a). Thus, with subtlety and irony, Socrates is saying that even at the end of the road one will be able to have fully before one's vision only an image of the truth itself, not the truth in its undivided, full luminosity. Or, to speak more directly, there is no end of the road, no haven where one would finally have the highest idea present without reserve before one's vision. Always there would remain images, difference—that is, the bond to concealment.

Once Plato's other beginning is allowed to come into play, one might again—though differently—radicalize and ironize the ancient tradition about Plato's unwritten teachings, about the unsaid of Plato's text. Now one might well take λήθη, concealment, to be this unsaid. This would not be an unsaid that could just as easily—or at least without too much difficulty—have been said. It is not that Plato somehow just neglected to say it. Rather, it remains unsaid because it resists saying, because it borders on the unsayable, because it withdraws from λόγος, refuses to submit to the question: τί ἐστι?, "What is . . . ?" And yet, it is not simply unsayable but is somehow inscribed, is the unsaid *of* Plato's text.

In what one might be tempted to take as Heidegger's last word on Plato, he tells of one of the ways in which this unsaid, λήθη, came to be inscribed by the Greeks. In his lecture course *Parmenides*, Heidegger says: "The last word of the Greeks that names λήθη in its essence is the μῦθος concluding Plato's dialogue on the essence of the polis."[7]

And yet, we know that this μῦθος is not merely a story told at the end of the dialogue, that it does not merely conclude the *Republic* as something added on at the end. Rather, this μῦθος is in play throughout the dialogue, in virtually all that is said and done in the course of the dialogue. It will, then, have installed λήθη everywhere, not only in the central images and figures of the dialogue, but from the very moment Socrates, beginning his narration—beginning thus again—says: "I went down yesterday to Piraeus. . . ."

7. Heidegger, *Parmenides*, 140.

2

The Place of the Good

What are the conditions, the presuppositions, under which discourse can legitimately ascribe a place to the good? Can the good be said to occupy a place? Can it be said to occur at some determinate place or other? Or is it only that it can be instantiated at some particular place, in some person or act that happens to be located at some particular place? Can the good be said to take place as such and not only in its instantiations? Or must it be said that the good as such is nowhere, that it comes to be somewhere only insofar as it ceases being the good as such and comes to be instantiated in something particular? In this case, one might go still further and invoke the venerable principle that whatever *is* is good precisely insofar as it *is*: then it could be said that, like being itself, the good is both nowhere and everywhere, lacking any determinate relation to place.

And yet—it will be asked—can the good be said *to be* anywhere? Can it be said even *to be* nowhere and everywhere? Can it be said *to be* at all? Or is it not *beyond being,* as was once said, indeed in the discourse that first forged the very possibility of such determinations of being and of the good? Even the most minimal declaration suffices already to display how such discourse cannot but work against itself, declaring at once the *is* and the surpassing of it, giving in one moment what it withdraws in another, imitating in this way the very movement, the effect, that—in that ancient discourse—the good is said to exercise.

Yet, even granting the retreat of the *is*, how can it be said that the good is nowhere and everywhere, considering that it is said to be precisely *beyond being*? How can the good be (yet also without being) *beyond* being otherwise than by sustaining a determinate relation to place? Yet what is this place beyond being? What sense can *place* have in this case, assuming—though it is not self-evident—that the determination of place is a matter of delimiting its sense?

Can these questions perhaps be addressed only if it is first determined what the good is? Would this not be the proper beginning? It would be, no doubt—this is almost always how one makes a proper beginning, by asking "What is . . . ?"—were it not that in this case such recourse recoils upon itself. For to ask "What is . . . ?" is to presuppose both the *what* and the *is,* whereas the ancient, founding discourse declares the good *beyond being*; and it determines the good as that which first enables the *what* and as that which therefore first makes it possible to interrogate things by asking *what* they are.

Questioning about the place of the good cannot, then, but coil back upon itself. It cannot but engage in granting, in letting withdraw, and in letting itself be drawn into the withdrawal, drawn along in it. This double spiraling will animate it as it unfolds all that lies in its questions: How, from the place beyond being, does the good bestow on things the possibility of being what they are? And how, from its place beyond being, does it grant to humans the vision by which to comprehend what things are, by which to apprehend them in their proper being?

>>><<<

The singularity of the Platonic dialogues complicates their interpretation. To read even just two such irreducibly singular texts together as if they were purely homogeneous cannot but prove reductive and distortive. To read them without regard for their heterogeneities cannot but disturb the intricate and delicate web within which each dialogue, in its own way, brings something to light. There is nothing more inconsequential than an interpretive discourse that proceeds by merely juxtaposing passages from different dialogues as if they belonged to the same dialogue or even to perfectly homogeneous segments of that single dialogue. As long as no questions are asked about such textually uncritical procedures, as long as no restrictions are set in place so as to govern the interpretive movement between dialogues and between different segments of the same dialogue, there will be virtually no limit to what Plato can be shown to have said, as if, in the dialogues, Plato ever said anything.

How, then, is it possible to read Platonic dialogues together in a way that is both critical and productive? What needs, above all, to be stressed can perhaps best be expressed by a word found often in these texts, the word χαλεπόν, which means *difficult, troublesome,* even *dangerous.* How, then, are these texts to be brought into contact? How is one dialogue—or even a brief segment of it—to be brought to bear critically and productively on another dialogue? What is the difficulty, the trouble, with which one must deal in such an interpretive endeavor? What is the danger to which one is thereby exposed?

What makes the going difficult is that one must take the trouble to demonstrate the dramatic and thematic connection between the dialogues that would be drawn together in the interpretation. The very difficulty of doing so—that is, the dramatic and thematic complexity of the dialogues—exposes the interpreter to the danger of failing to discern heterogeneities, discontinuities, that, despite all affinities, set the texts apart. Yet there are most certainly cases where an intimate connection can be demonstrated directly from the texts themselves. For instance, the *Theaetetus,* the *Sophist,* and the *Statesman* are linked by an internal chronology that makes them almost a single conversation, begun one day and continued early on the following day; they are also linked by the fact that those present at the scene of the conversation remain the same, except that on the second day the others are joined by the Stranger from Elea. Though it is more subtle, there is also considerable thematic continuity between the three dialogues, for instance, in their common focus on questions concerning λόγος. Nonetheless, as one moves through these dialogues, perspectives shift and questions evolve, as different persons assume the roles of speaker and of respondent. Though these three dialogues can—and ultimately even must—be read together, merely juxtaposing various passages without mediation would be out of the question. Rather, everything would depend on the mediation, which would require letting the difference of context remain in play even as disparate passages are brought together.

The connection between the *Timaeus* and the *Republic* is more complicated, and interpretive movement between these two dialogues is consequently more problematic. At the beginning of the *Timaeus* Socrates refers to their conversation of yesterday, noting that three of the others involved—though not the fourth—are now present. Timaeus asks Socrates to help them recall that conversation. Socrates' recapitulation identifies yesterday's conversation as having concerned the kind of constitution (πολιτεία) that would prove best. He recalls that they began by assigning to each citizen his one proper τέχνη and then proceeded by distinguishing from all others those who would serve as guardians of the city. The latter, Socrates says, would need to have souls that are, to the highest degree, both spirited and philosophic. Both male and female guardians, who are to be treated equally, must be trained in gymnastic and music. They are to have all things in common, even as regards marriages and child-production. All are to regard all as their actual kinsmen, though the rulers are to contrive that the best mate with the best.

The thematic connection with the *Republic* could hardly be more apparent. Everything suggests that, in and as the beginning of the *Timaeus*, Socrates is recapitulating the building of cities in λόγος that occupies most of Books 2–5 of the *Republic*. There is a long tradition, which goes back at least to Proclus and extends up through Thomas Taylor and Henri Martin, according to which the *Republic* is taken to be precisely that discourse of yesterday that Socrates recapitulates in the *Timaeus*. Proclus, for instance, notes that the events of the *Republic* take place on the Bendideia and that the *Timaeus* marks itself as occurring on the festival day of Athena (see *Tim.* 26e). Assuming that this festival day is the Lesser Panathenaea, Proclus proposes that these two dialogues involve a sequence of three days. On the first day the events reported in the *Republic* take place; this is the day of the Bendideia when Socrates and Glaucon go down to Piraeus and engage until late that night in the conversation in the house of Polemarchus. On the second day Socrates tells about the events and conversation that took place on the previous day; back in Athens, he narrates the entire discussion to Timaeus, Critias, Hermocrates, and the unnamed fourth mentioned at the beginning of the *Timaeus*. It is this narration that constitutes the text of the *Republic*, though of course that text identifies only the narrator Socrates and not those to whom he tells the story. Then, on the third day, the festival day of Athena, Socrates recapitulates the narrative for Timaeus, Critias, and Hermocrates, and this recapitulation is followed by the rest of the discourses belonging to the *Timaeus*.

Such a strong dramatic connection, that the *Timaeus* not only is set the day after the *Republic* but even begins by recapitulating the *Republic*, is not to be found between any other dialogues.[1] Even taking into account the fact that what is actually recapitulated is only the building of cities in λόγος and so includes neither the discourse on their corruption nor the central digression on the philosopher, this remarkable dramatic and thematic overlap could be taken as a basis for bringing one of the dialogues to bear—even decisively—on the other.

<hr>

1. In addition to the *Theaetetus*, the *Sophist*, and the *Statesman*, in which the temporal continuity is explicitly indicated (see *Pol.* 258a), there are other dialogues that are connected by internal chronology, perhaps most notably those set during the time of the trial, imprisonment, and death of Socrates (hence, the *Euthyphro*, the *Apology*, the *Crito*, and the *Phaedo*). Likewise, the beginning of the *Critias* is such as to suggest that the conversation there follows immediately upon the completion of that presented in the *Timaeus*. What—even despite the chronological complications still to be discussed—makes the connection between the *Republic* and the *Timaeus* remarkable, if not indeed unique, is that the *Timaeus* includes a recapitulation of a large segment of the *Republic*.

Yet, regrettably, the connection is more tenuous than it appeared to Proclus and those who followed him. Later scholars have established that the Lesser (and Greater) Panathenaea did not in fact come right after the Bendideia but two months later. Therefore, recent commentators either abandon entirely the supposition of a three-day sequence and take the *Timaeus* to occur on the Greater or Lesser Panathenaea; or they take the relevant festival of Athena to be some other festival such as the Plynteria, though even this, it seems, occurred five days after the Bendideia.[2]

Even if the precise dramatic connection is less than certain, the remarkable thematic overlap remains. Though mediation and discretion will be imperative in spacing the respective discourses, there is a basis—even, one might say, a provocation—to bring certain moves ventured in the *Timaeus* to bear on the *Republic*, especially if there should turn out to be places where the text of the *Republic* itself invites such recourse.

>>><<<

Book 7 of the *Republic* begins deep inside the cave where, in the dim light, the prisoners, unaware of their bondage, contend with one another regarding the fleeting shadows that pass before them. In the course of Book 7, Socrates both describes and, with Glaucon, enacts the ascent from the cave into the open expanse above. Indeed he describes and enacts the ascent several times, Book 7 consisting precisely of the initial account and this series of repetitions. Yet, for all the elaboration brought by these repetitions, none are so decisive as the initial account in which Socrates unfolds the image of the cave; and, within this account, nothing is more decisive than the passage—a single sentence— that describes the final stage of the ascent. How one reads this sentence will determine how one interprets the entirety of Book 7, if not indeed the entirety of the *Republic*.

2. See my discussion of the relation between the *Republic* and the *Timaeus* in *Chorology: On Beginning in Plato's "Timaeus"* (Bloomington: Indiana University Press, 1999), 21–23.

The context of this sentence has first of all to be reconstituted, or—as Socrates would say—recapitulated.

Book 7 begins with Socrates proposing to make an image (ἀπεικάζω) of our nature (φύσις) with regard to education (παιδεία) and the lack thereof. The performative character of the discussion is such that the entire passage, including the sentence in question, consists in deed in Socrates' making an image, in his engagement in image-making. That what he makes is an image of our nature with regard to education is not unproblematic: for it will turn out that education consists precisely in the soul's turning around from that to which it is by nature oriented, indeed in its turning around from nature as such.

The image that Socrates makes—as an image *of* our nature with regard to education—is that of humans in a subterranean cave. This most recounted, most familiar—but also thereby most sedimented, most taken for granted—discourse tells of prisoners chained in the cave in such a way that they see and hear only the shadows cast on the inner wall before them. The shadows are cast by artifacts carried like puppets along the parapet behind them; a fire farther up, behind the parapet, provides the dim light that illuminates the cave and allows the shadows to appear. Those carrying the artifacts across are thus the ones who determine what counts as being true in this subterranean city, itself an image of every city. Note indeed that when Glaucon calls both this image and these prisoners, as he puts it, strange, out of place (ἄτοπος), Socrates simply replies, "They're like us" (*Rep.* 515a); and then, as if to explain this similarity, he goes on to observe that the prisoners would not have seen anything of themselves or of one another except the shadows cast on the wall of the cave, their ignorance of self and other thus corresponding, he implies, to our own.

Socrates not only makes the image but also tells the story of certain events that take place in this setting; indeed telling the story is his way of carrying on the image-making still further, for it is precisely in the story that the rest of the image, the other region conjoined to the subterranean cave, takes shape. The story tells of the release of a prisoner and of the course he follows after his release. More precisely, the story describes the form that his release (λύσις) and his healing (ἴασις) from bonds would take if something of this sort were by nature (φύσει) to happen to him. The reference to nature in this description is striking, since it turns out that the healing consists in that same turning away from nature that also constitutes education. How can one come by nature to turn away from nature? The story goes on to indicate that in a sense one cannot; that is, Socrates goes on to refer to another, to the teacher—and the self-reference soon becomes explicit—who compels the prisoner to stand up and turn around and to answer his questions about what things are and who even drags him along on the upward way. What would have happened to the prisoner merely by nature would not, it seems, have sufficed to produce the release and the turning away from nature. Rather, for such healing and education the teacher is needed. Nature, it seems, can only have produced in the prisoner a certain receptiveness to the teacher, a receptiveness that nonetheless does not lack resistance. This receptiveness would lie in a certain intimation of a "beyond." However ambivalent, the prisoner would, from within nature, have gained a certain directedness beyond nature. Within the prisoner the eruption of a certain monstrosity would have made him receptive—even though still resistant—to the Socratic teacher.[3]

The story tells how the prisoner, once he is released, is pained and bedazzled and how, consequently, he would resist turning around toward the light. It tells then of what would happen if he were dragged away onto the upward way and out into the light of the sun, of how at first he would be blinded by the intense light and would be unable to see any of the things there above.

---

3. This reference to nature has been variously interpreted, sometimes in the sense of something happening "in the course of nature," sometimes in the sense of something that happens "no one knows how." Adam explains the reference by reversing the value of nature: the condition of the prisoners in the darkness of the cave he takes as unnatural. He concludes: "Their release is therefore a return to their true nature, and may for this reason be described as 'natural.' This, I think, is what Plato means to suggest by φύσει" (Adam, *The Republic of Plato*, 2:91 n. 18).

Socrates tells of how then, gradually, he would grow accustomed to the brightness, first discerning shadows, then the reflections of humans and of other things in water, and later the things themselves. Then, Socrates continues, he could go on to behold the things in heaven and the heaven itself, more easily at night by the light of the stars and the moon than in daytime by the sun and its light.

This narrative provides the immediate context for the decisive passage that, in turn, supplies the capstone of the entire story of the cave. Indeed, in telling how the prisoner is led up out of the cave, the entirety of Book 7 up to this point itself leads up to the single sentence in which Socrates describes the final stage of the ascent. The sentence follows immediately upon Glaucon's ratification of what has just been said. In a conventional translation, which will require commentary and even countertranslation, the sentence—voiced by Socrates—reads: "Then finally I suppose he would be able to look upon the sun, not its appearance in water or in some alien abode, but the sun itself by itself in its own place and to behold how it is" (*Rep.* 516b). It is not insignificant that Socrates voices this description not as an assertion but as a supposition: that the escaped prisoner would be able to look upon the sun in this way is something Socrates supposes or believes; it is what he would anticipate or expect, all these senses being conveyed by the word οἶμαι. That Socrates expresses something supposed or expected rather than known is indicative of the limitation under which the discourse of the *Republic* proceeds, even where, as in Book 7, it reaches its highest point.[4]

At the final stage of the ascent what occurs is a looking upon and a beholding. This occurrence only brings to completion what has occurred at every stage of the ascent and at every stage of the narrative that tells of the ascent. Throughout the ascent and throughout the narrative about it, the concern is always with looking upon something, with beholding how something is—that is, it is always a matter of seeing. As soon as Socrates instructs

---

4. See my discussion in *Being and Logos*, 440f.

Glaucon to make an image, the imperative is that he see the image—as we say—with the mind's eye, that, as he forms it, he bring the image before his inner vision, before what in subsequent Greek thought will be called φαντασία. Then, immediately continuing, Socrates instructs him: "See [ἰδέ] human beings as though they were in an underground cave-like dwelling..." (*Rep.* 514a). When Socrates has finished his initial description of this dwelling, Glaucon replies: "I see [ὁρῶ]." Then, immediately, Socrates continues: "So then, see [ὅρα τοίνυν] along this wall human beings carrying all sorts of artifacts..." (*Rep.* 514b). When Glaucon remarks on the strangeness of the image, Socrates turns to speaking of what those in the cave themselves see. They see, so he says, only the shadows cast on the inside wall of the cave; and if they were to engage in discussion, they would take the names they utter to refer to the passing shadows, just as they would attribute to these shadows any sounds that they might hear.

With the description of the cave-like dwelling completed, Socrates turns to the story of what happens once a prisoner is released. Here again what Socrates asks of Glaucon is that he behold, look upon (σκόπει)—that is, see in his mind's eye—the course followed once the prisoner is released. That course is, in turn, one of seeing, of looking up toward the light, though indeed at the cost of being pained and dazzled; it is a matter then of looking at the light itself; and then, dragged from the cave, it is a matter of emerging into the light of the sun and of being still more dazzled by the brightness. Then the escaped prisoner would come to see shadows and reflections, then gradually even things themselves; and eventually he would turn his vision upward to the heaven, at first by night, then finally by day, looking upon the sun itself. At all these stages, but most of all in looking upon the sun itself, the power of sight would, as Socrates will soon declare, imitate another beholding, one raised to the level of dialectic (see *Rep.* 532a). The force of the image and story of the cave derives from this imitative capacity that belongs to the power of sight.

The story of the cave not only opens upon the whole of Book 7 but in a sense constitutes it in its entirety. For what follows in

Book 7 is a series of repetitions of the story. In each of the seven repetitions, which are distinctly articulated, there is a certain emphasis by which the initial story comes to be reshaped as it is retold. The first repetition (517a–18c) reiterates the ascent from the cave in such a way as to connect it explicitly with the figure of the divided line elaborated at the end of Book 6. This connection serves to make it explicit also that looking upon the sun itself by itself corresponds to seeing the idea of the good. The second repetition (518c–19b) returns to the theme of education and, now presenting the ascent precisely as a turning around (περιαγωγή) of the entire soul, describes education as the drawing out of the sight present in the soul such that just such a turning around of the soul is produced. The third repetition (519b–21c), affirming the ascent of education, lets the problematic relation of philosophy to politics reemerge. Thus, granting the ascent (ἀνάβασις) to a seeing of the good, the emphasis is shifted to the descent (κατάβασις), to the necessity of compelling the "best natures" (those who by nature most exceed mere nature) to go down from what seems like the Isles of the Blessed into the city. Thus would those least eager to rule come to govern in the way that is best.

The fourth repetition (521c–32b) is the most extensive. Here again the story of the cave is told, that is, the story of the ascent culminating in the beholding of the sun/good. But now the emphasis is on education, not just education in its general character as a turning around of the soul, but education as it would be effected through various studies, in particular, through the mathematical disciplines, which convey the soul beyond the level achievable through the mere curriculum of gymnastic and music prescribed earlier in the *Republic*. The ascent to the light—"just as some men are said to have gone from Hades up to the gods" (*Rep.* 521c)[5]—is to be accomplished by progression through the mathematical disciplines, from arithmetic to harmonics; this progression, in turn,

---

5. This remark, whatever its specific reference (see Adam [*Republic of Plato*, 2:105] who mentions several possibilities), serves most significantly to reinscribe in the λόγος at this point the μῦθος that runs throughout the entire dialogue from its opening sentence to the concluding myth of Er (see *Being and Logos*, 313–20).

is to provide the prelude to dialectic, and it is through dialectic that one would come finally to look upon the sun/good.

The fifth repetition (532b–33e), though condensed, is quite close to the initial story itself. One remarkable feature in this repetition is Glaucon's observation that repetition—precisely such repetition as is here being carried out—is necessary ("since it's not only now that these things must be heard, but they must all be returned to many times in the future" [*Rep.* 532d]). Equally remarkable, indeed even more consequential in confirming the limited perspective of the discourse, is Socrates' refusal, when Glaucon requests it, to go on to the end of the journey. To Glaucon's request, Socrates answers: "You would no longer be able to follow, my dear Glaucon" (*Rep.* 533a).

The sixth, penultimate repetition (533e–35a) reiterates the fourfold division on the line, thus again connecting the story of the cave to the figure of the line, now fixing the designations of the various segments (ἐπιστήμη, διάνοια, πίστις, εἰκασία). The final repetition (535a–41b) returns to the survey of the course of studies in order to determine their distribution. As he prescribes the age at which those chosen are to take up each of the studies, Socrates recapitulates once more the story of the ascent.

>>><<<

If, for the time being, we stay with the image itself, deferring the eikastic passage that will eventually be needed in order, through the image, to discern—and thus to enact—the soul's proper ascent, then the content of the story, the locale especially of its culmination, draws our attention to the discussion of astronomy found near the middle of Book 7. This discussion occurs in the fourth repetition of the story of the cave; it constitutes the penultimate stage in the extended account of the mathematical disciplines that are to belong to the curriculum prescribed for the philosopher-guardians. The entire account is marked by a peculiar duplicity (in the double sense) as a result of the twofold demand issued, the demand both for ascent and for the appropriate, subsequent descent. Specifically, the account proposes to show that the disciplines in question are such that, on the one hand, they will serve to turn the soul around and draw it upward toward being and, on the other hand, they will prove useful to the guardians in war.

In the case of astronomy, in particular, usefulness in warfare is merely mentioned in passing. Indeed it is as if, in the progression through the mathematical disciplines, either they prove less and less useful in war or Socrates and Glaucon become more and more oblivious to whatever such use they might have. In fact, when they come to discuss the last of these disciplines, harmonics, they declare, without apology, that it is useless except in its capacity to draw the soul upward toward the beautiful and the good. Thus the curriculum turns out to be geared primarily to the education of the philosopher rather than the guardian-ruler. This drift away from the latter only serves to emphasize again—though now in a different and perhaps more decisive way—that the paradox of the philosopher-ruler borders on the aporetic. The drift is completed in the discussion of dialectic, in which there is complete silence regarding usefulness in war. The almost aporetic conclusion of Book 7 should come, then, as no surprise. Socrates assures Glaucon that the things they have said about the city are "not in every way prayers." These things are, he says, "difficult" (χαλεπόν—so also: troublesome, dangerous); but, he continues, they are "in some way possible" (*Rep.* 540d). Yet, when Socrates goes on to specify the way, saying indeed that there is no other way, he declares that philosophers, those who are truly philosophers, must come to power in a city. Most conspicuously, there is no mention of guardians nor—as in earlier formulations—of guardians or rulers becoming philosophers. Socrates' account of the means by which the philosophers who have come to power could bring about the city that has been described only serves to stress how difficult the task is, how dangerous, how aporetic, how unlikely it is that it will become anything more than a prayer: for their only recourse is to expel from the city in which they come to power all who are older than ten, beginning thus with what is merely a city of children, of philosophers and children.

We proposed to stay, for a time, with the mere image depicting the escaped prisoner as he comes to look upon the sun itself. Thus we were drawn to the discussion of astronomy—only then to be drawn on, as if driven by a swift current or swept away by a mighty wave, into an ascendancy that virtually outstrips the concerns of the guardians. Such being swept away, being drawn into the ascent beyond the city, is the deed (ἔργον) being enacted, and it is—as just now attested—a deed deeply etched in the text of the central Books, especially Book 7. What Socrates calls the biggest of the three waves—the driving forces of the central digression—proves still more powerful than its initial depiction—as the paradox of the philosopher-king—would suggest. It is this wave that carries the philosopher on beyond and that sweeps the discourse along to that end, at the end of Book 7, where the philosopher is left ruling over a city of children.

It also sweeps the image along toward what is more original—indeed to such an extent that resistance to its force inevitably generates comedy. This is precisely what happens in the discussion of astronomy. As with the other curricular discussions, the aim here is to show that, above and beyond its rather meager usefulness in war, astronomy also serves to turn the soul upward toward being. Glaucon exclaims with confidence that astronomy has precisely this effect: "In my opinion it's evident to everyone that astronomy compels the soul to see what's above and leads it there away from the things here" (*Rep.* 529a). Socrates is not long letting the little comedy unfold. He expresses his disagreement with Glaucon's exclamation and insists that, in the hands of those who now pursue it, astronomy causes the soul to look downward, not upward. Socrates compares the Glauconian astronomer to one who sets out to learn about things above by tilting his head back and looking at decorations on a ceiling. Or, in another, no less ludicrous image, this astronomer is like one who thinks he can learn about such things by floating on his back on land or sea. The point of the little comedy is that one must carry out the dianoetic passage from the decorations in the heaven to the numbers, figures, and motions that are imaged by what is visible in the heaven. Only then, only when the decorations in the heaven are used as patterns for the sake of learning of these other things accessible only to λόγος and thought, only then is astronomy properly pursued. And then, says Socrates, we will let the things in the heaven go, will let them alone. Astronomy would aim, then, at having nothing to do with beholding the starry heaven. It would direct our look up to the heaven in order that we might look beyond the heaven. It would turn to the things in the heaven in order to let these things go, teaching us to let them alone.

It is precisely such astronomy, together with harmonics as similarly described, that is carried out in the *Timaeus*. In the first of his three discourses, Timaeus works out the sequence of numbers or ratios according to which—in the poietic idiom of the dialogue—the god harmoniously articulated the long band that was to become the soul of the cosmos. Once it had been thus partitioned, the god split the band lengthwise and formed the two resulting bands into intersecting circles or rings set obliquely to each other and revolving in opposite directions. One circle represents the movement of the fixed stars. The other circle the god split in six places so as to form seven unequal circles, which he then arranged according to the squares and cubes in the series of odd and even numbers (thus: 1, 2, 3, 4, 8, 9, 27); these represent the movement of the sun, moon, and planets. Though cast as an account of godly ποίησις, what Timaeus is describing are those true numbers, figures, and motions of which Socrates speaks in the *Republic*. The point is reinforced by Timaeus' insistence that these circles in the cosmic soul represent only the motion or orbits of the heavenly bodies, not those bodies themselves, which only much later in the godly ποίησις will be set in the orbits. At the stage where the circles have just been formed, Timaeus states explicitly that the soul that has been generated is invisible. At this stage the starry heaven itself, the visible cosmos, has yet to appear. In the Socratic idiom of the *Republic,* the things in the heaven have been let go, let alone. In the idiom of the *Timaeus,* this astronomy is such as to concern only the work of νοῦς.

And yet, as Timaeus' first discourse approaches its end, a certain dissonance becomes audible. Indeed precisely at the moment of greatest ascendancy, at the moment when Timaeus tells of our vision of the heaven and of how that vision has endowed us with number and with philosophy itself, at this moment he has to acknowledge that there are also certain causes, linked to the elements, that are not the work of νοῦς and that accordingly cannot be let alone and replaced by the true numbers, figures, and motions. It is the intrusion of these anoetic elements that forces Timaeus to break off his first discourse and to launch a new beginning.

Suffice it to say that in the discourse that then follows, the breach just opened is extended into a fundamental ontological reorientation. What comes to operate is no longer the merely twofold distinction between intelligible and sensible but rather a threefold schema. The third kind, to which Timaeus' second discourse is largely devoted, is depicted in several ways, by means of several names. But its proper name—if it can indeed have a proper name—is χώρα. Timaeus says of the χώρα that it grants an abode (ἕδρα) to all things that are generated, that is, to everything sensible. Only inasmuch as such images, such phantoms, are generated in the χώρα, can they, as Timaeus says, cling "to being at least in a certain way, on pain of being nothing at all" (*Tim.* 52c).[6]

>>><<<

Let us turn back to the *Republic,* to the image of the escaped prisoner as he comes finally to turn his vision upward to the diurnal heaven so as to look upon the sun itself. Note, then, that this image is remarkably similar to the one at the end of Timaeus' first discourse, that of one who turns his vision upward to the heaven in a way that would in a sense consummate philosophy but that also first opens the breach that leads eventually to the χώρα. Could it be that the force of the biggest wave is even greater than suspected? Could it be that its force is such as to

6. See *Chorology*, chap. 2–3.

sweep all of us along not only from the image to the intelligible that it images but also on toward the χώρα, which first grants an abode for images?

In any case there is something very curious, indeed disturbing, about the image depicting the escaped prisoner looking upon the sun itself, something that could not go unnoticed and cannot be passed over: one could look upon the sun itself only at the cost of ruining one's eyes, blinding oneself. A vision of the sun itself would lead to the extinguishing of vision. Rather than making it possible for all things to appear in their truth, to show themselves unconcealedly as what they are, looking upon the sun itself would have the effect of sealing the would-be visionary in a blindness to which nothing could appear; precisely as a result of his looking upon the sun, all things would be withdrawn into utter concealment.

It is remarkable that in the *Republic* no mention is made of the blindness that would result from looking upon the sun, though, in interpreting the repeated reference to such vision, one cannot merely pass over this circumstance. One might be tempted to turn to the celebrated passage in the *Phaedo* in which again there is reference to looking upon the sun (specifically during an eclipse) but also, in contrast to the *Republic*, mention of the blindness that can result. The contrast between this passage and the corresponding passages in the *Republic* is further extended by the conclusion that is drawn: not, as in the *Republic*, that one should strive to look upon the sun, but rather quite the contrary, that one should turn away and have recourse to some other means by which to discover the truth of things. Not only the contexts but also the very sense and direction of the passages in the two dialogues are so thoroughly different that the most attentive and intricate mediation would be required in order to read them together.[7]

Yet, quite aside from the warning issued by the passage in the *Phaedo*, it cannot go unremarked, purely in the context of the

---

7. I will return to the question of reading these passages together in the course of the discussion with Derrida in chapter 3.

Republic, that vision of the sun itself extinguishes vision, produces blindness—or rather, that it does so unless, as we normally and regularly do, one merely glances momentarily at the sun. Is it perhaps only such a momentary glance at the sun that the escaped prisoner would venture?

But, however it may be with the image itself, what counts is that which the image images, the intelligible sense to which we are in any case swept along by the biggest of the waves. In fact, as soon as Socrates has finished his image-making endeavor and has told of what befalls the escaped prisoner upon his return to the cave, he turns to the first repetition, in which he explains the image by connecting it explicitly with the previous discourses, especially that of the divided line. Here he confirms what one would in any case suppose on the basis of the analogy drawn in Book 6 between the sun and the good. Though Socrates is careful to mark the limitation of his perspective, the explanation could hardly be more explicit: "This is the way the phenomena look to me: in the knowable (ἐν τῷ γνωστῷ) the last thing to be seen, and scarcely, is the idea of the good" (*Rep.* 517b–c). What is most remarkable in this passage is not just that it identifies the idea of the good as what is imaged by the sun but also, surprisingly perhaps, that it marks the seeing of this last thing as something *scarcely* accomplished. The word that I have translated as *scarcely,* the adverb μόγις, means, first of all, *with toil and trouble* and then, consequently, *hardly* or *scarcely.* The sense is that whatever requires toil and trouble for its accomplishment will hardly, scarcely, be accomplished. It is imperative to retain both senses: the final vision requires toil and trouble, is difficult, troublesome, dangerous, and therefore it is, at best, just scarcely achieved, just barely.

Mere reference back to the relevant discussion in Book 6 suffices to indicate why the culminating vision of the idea of the good is difficult, why it requires toil and trouble. For, since the idea of the good is, as Socrates declares, "beyond being, exceeding it in rank and power" (*Rep.* 509b), vision of it requires that we see farther than in every other instance; the vision required must extend over and beyond everything that is and reach an abode utterly beyond being. It is not surprising therefore that Glaucon swears in response to Socrates' declaration: "And Glaucon, quite ridiculously, said, 'Apollo, what a daimonic excess'" (*Rep.* 509c).

But what is this abode beyond being? The question is of course entirely improper, for if this abode is beyond being then it neither simply *is* nor is a *what*. Its excess sets it beyond such questions, and this no doubt is why, with the phrase "quite ridiculously" (μάλα γελοίως) Socrates hints at a certain proximity to comedy, such comedy as would ensue if one were forgetful of the excess, forgetful that discourse constantly risks being exceeded here by what would be said.

What, then, about the abode beyond being? What is to be said about it? The most decisive saying about it in the *Republic* occurs in the sentence that, in the initial story of the cave, describes the final stage of the ascent. Here again is that sentence: "Then finally I suppose he would be able to look upon the sun, not its appearance in water or in some alien abode, but the sun itself by itself in its own place and to behold how it is." Now it needs to be made explicit that the word translated as *abode*, the word ἕδρα, is precisely the same word that is used when it is said in the *Timaeus* that the χώρα grants an abode to all generated things. In this passage it is a matter, then, not of looking upon the idea of the good in some abode that is alien, improper to it, but, as the passage goes on to say, of seeing it "itself by itself in its own place"—that is, as it actually says, dropping the impossible translation, "in its χώρα." It is a matter of seeing it "itself by itself in its χώρα." The culminating vision is a beholding of the idea of the good in its χώρα. In such a vision, says Socrates, one will behold how it is.

Does this mean, then, that the χώρα too is beyond being, even though Plato's texts never bring the expression ἐπέκεινα τῆς οὐσίας to bear on it? This is a question that Jacques Derrida posed in the course of our extended discussion of the *Timaeus*, the question as to why Plato forgoes saying that the χώρα is ἐπέκεινα τῆς οὐσίας, as to why saying and thinking this seems so difficult. In resuming the discussion with Derrida (in chapter 3),

I will return to this question. For now, let it suffice to respond merely by observing that the χώρα is rigorously differentiated from everything that in any way *is*, both from the intelligible ideas and from sensible things, and that to this extent it is beyond being. Or rather, it would perhaps be more suitable to say that it is before being. It is perhaps this difference that makes it difficult to say and to think the χώρα as beyond being. It also complicates the problem of understanding what is meant in referring to the idea of the good as "in its χώρα." Does this mean that its χώρα is the abode in which its operation is secured? Or does the χώρα, from before being, grant to the idea of the good its abode beyond being? And is its χώρα the same as the χώρα that grants an abode to generated, sensible things?

Though these immeasurably difficult questions must be heeded or at least voiced, the present danger is that this even mightier wave may sweep us on past that single sentence on which our sights have been set from the beginning and for the sake of which we have ventured into the depths. For the primary question that this sentence prompts concerns, on the one hand, the character of the looking that occurs when one looks upon the idea of the good and, on the other hand, the way in which the idea of the good shows itself to such a looking. What is the look of the good when one looks upon it?

The character of the culminating look can best be determined by focusing first of all on that point on the upward way where thought or intellect (διάνοια, νόησις) is first called forth, the point at which one moves decisively beyond sense. In Book 7, at the outset of the fourth repetition, Socrates presents an account of this transition, and this account provides the basis for his discussion of the philosophical curriculum. Socrates begins by observing that some things perceived by sense do not summon the intellect whereas some others do. The ones that do have this effect of summoning intellect Socrates describes as those that "go over to the opposite perception" in such a way that "the perception doesn't reveal one thing any more than its opposite" (*Rep.* 523c). Thus, he notes, the mere perception of a finger is not likely to arouse thought; yet if one and the same finger is felt as both hard and soft or if the index finger appears both shorter (than the middle finger) and longer (than the little finger), then the soul is at a loss (ἀπορέω) about the object, is thrown into an aporia. Socrates describes how thought then awakens: in such a case the soul brings calculation and intellect into play and "tries to determine whether each of the things reported to it is one or two" (*Rep.* 524b). Then, he continues, if each—for instance, hard and soft—is one and both are two, "the soul will think the two as separate," in contrast to their manner of being mixed up together in perception. Thus, what thought does is to posit, over against the mixing-up of opposites in sense, the various determinations in their oneness and distinctness. Most remarkably, Socrates concludes: "And so, it was on this ground that we called the one intelligible and the other visible" (*Rep.* 524c). Because, in its ascent from the sensible into the intelligible, thought aims precisely at these ones, the appropriate study for the philosopher is mathematics, and, to begin with, arithmetic, which has as its subject matter the pure, indistinguishable ones involved in counting and hence in number as the Greeks understood it. Yet even far beyond the level of the mathematical disciplines, intellect remains oriented to ones; even where it becomes a question of a community (κοινωνία) between them, as in the discussion of the five kinds in the *Sophist*, these kinds remain distinct ones.

At all these levels the character of the looking effected through thought remains the same: it is a matter of looking toward a one, of coming to look upon a one look, as in the passage through images someone can come to look upon the one original they image. What is preeminent, then, in that upon which one would come to look is its character as a one, as a one, distinct look.

The question is whether the character of the looking and of the looked upon remain unchanged in the passage to the consummating vision of the idea of the good.

When, in Book 6, Socrates draws the analogy between the sun and the good, he calls the sun the offspring or son (male progeny) (ἔκγονος) of the good, and he says that this offspring is "most similar" to its father. Thus, the sun is characterized as something like an image of the good, an image of the good begotten by the good itself. Though Socrates does not say at this point whether there are other children of the good, his remark suffices to indicate that the good engages in image-making, in erotically making images of itself that are sent forth even into the realm of sense. The subsequent discussion of the good as providing both the truth and especially the being of things—of intelligibles— suggests, without the erotic imagery, that all such things, all intelligible ideas, are children of the good, progeny brought forth in its image, through its image-making.

Yet what preeminently renders these progeny intelligible is that each is one. Each is a being itself, and, as being itself, it is one and the same as itself. To say that the good bestows being upon the knowables (that is, the intelligibles) is to say precisely that it grants to each its distinct oneness. Constituted as one with itself, each is such that it need not show itself only mixed up with others that it is not; rather, each can show itself as it is, in its being one with itself; and it can show itself openly and unconcealedly, that is, truly, in the original sense of ἀλήθεια.

As one ascends toward the vision of the good, one will be offered a certain intimation by way of the images that the good will have made of itself and put forth that they might be seen by those on the upward way. The question—the question of all questions— is whether, passing through these images of the good by the good, one comes finally to look upon the good itself beyond all images; or whether, at the very moment when one comes to look upon it, it withdraws and deflects one's vision back to the images it has fathered.

I will not insist that a definitive answer to this question is offered in Book 7 or anywhere else in the *Republic*. Whether the discourse of this dialogue is even such as to provide the conditions of possibility of anything like a definitive answer to this question is itself highly questionable. And yet—though stopping short of decisiveness—there is much in Book 7 to suggest that no sustained consummating vision can occur. One instance is the passage in which Socrates responds to Glaucon's eagerness to get on to the end of the journey that began with the prisoner's release and that, as Socrates tells of it, is also being enacted in the discourse he and Glaucon are carrying on. Socrates says: "You will no longer be able to follow, my dear Glaucon . . . , although there wouldn't be any lack of eagerness on my part. But you would no longer be seeing an image of what we are saying, but rather the truth itself, at least as it looks to me" (*Rep.* 533a). Note that Socrates not only refuses to move on to this vision but, as if enacting the very deflection of vision from it, qualifies what he says by the phrase "at least as it looks to me," that is, in the image it presents to him.

Yet no passage is more suggestive in this respect than the single sentence to which once more we return, the sentence that depicts the escaped prisoner looking upon the sun in its χώρα. For, if indeed looking upon the good is like looking upon the sun in its χώρα, then most assuredly one can effect no more than a momentary glance at it.[8] Except during an eclipse,[9] one cannot endure looking at it more than momentarily; one's vision is repulsed, or, to construe it from the other side, it withholds itself from our vision. Indeed it not only withdraws, escaping our direct vision, but also deflects that vision, temporarily injects blindness into it. As one turns away from the sun, blind spots remain before one's eyes. They are the most immediate images that the sun makes of itself.

That the idea of the good is to be seen only momentarily, that it turns away and deflects our vision, hints at the character of what in deed we look upon in this vision, this mere glimpse, of the good. For in this case the idea of the good—at least as it appears to our vision—could hardly be a paradigm, a model by which, once we had it thoroughly in mind, we could judge which things exemplify it and so are good. For we never get it thoroughly in mind,

---

8. It is significant that in this sentence the two verbs that denote the apprehending of the idea of the good occur as aorist infinitives (κατιδεῖν, θεάσασθαι), hence underlining the singleness, the noncontinuation, of the vision. The adverbial οἷος is appropriate in the same connection if taken to mean *how*, in distinction, for instance, from *what*.

9. Though in the *Republic* there is no mention of looking at the sun during an eclipse, this is precisely the condition that is explicit in the relevant passage in the *Phaedo*. For the interpretation of that passage, it is significant that, in looking at the sun during an eclipse, one would blind oneself without even the compensation of having enjoyed a full vision of the sun, which during an eclipse is hidden from view behind the moon.

and at this level the very paradigm of paradigm breaks down.[10] What, then, does one see in the momentary vision of the good? If we consider what precisely is said of the good, that it provides truth to the knowables and that it bestows the to-be (τὸ εἶναι) and being (οὐσία) upon the knowables, then one might suppose that in the momentary vision one catches a glimpse of this *giving,* even as the giver of the gift retreats. And then one might suppose, as well, that—as far as we humans can judge—what is good about the idea of the good is that it gives to things their being and truth. What is good about it is its generosity.[11]

In this case the χώρα, its χώρα, would be, then, the abode, the region, or, perhaps most appropriately, the spacing of the self-withholding, self-image-making generosity as which—and only as which—the good appears, indeed appears in its very retreat. It is this strange vision—utterly ἄτοπος—that would be had if, looking momentarily—ἐξαίφνης—upon the good, one would, as Socrates says, behold how it is.

---

10. To be sure, in the final repetition of the story of the cave, Socrates refers to those who have persevered throughout the entire course of education and speaks of them as "seeing the good itself and using it as a paradigm for ordering city, private men, and themselves" (*Rep.* 540a). Yet, even aside from the intrinsic reversibility of the word (a pattern can readily be construed as an example, as a copy or representation over against the original or pattern), παράδειγμα cannot be understood here as an eidetic model in the sense that presumably would hold for all other ideas. The good would be a paradigm only in the bestowals through which paradigms in the usual sense first become possible. This distinctiveness accorded to the good is perhaps what triggers the more conspicuous alternation in its designation, that it is called sometimes *the good,* sometimes *the idea of the good.*

11. It is in relation to this generosity—and not by bringing into play such modern concepts as value—that the goodness or excellence of things is to be understood. To give only the briefest indication: the excellence (ἀρετή) of something lies in its being what it is—as, for instance, an excellent knife is one that is such as to be capable of the cutting for which knives are designed. To be what it is—rather than being also other than what it is—is to be one and the same as itself. It is precisely this oneness that is bestowed by the good in its generosity. The good's bestowal of ἀλήθεια would need also to be taken into account, especially in the determination of the excellence of humans.

'the concept always demands sentences, discourses, work and
ss: text, in a word."[5] Even though the χώρα proves to be
ncept at all but rather turns out to withdraw from all con-
, from conceptuality as such, it too—indeed even more im-
gly—requires that discussion reinstall the word in its ex-
d context. Thus the discussion readily extended to other
gues, most notably, the *Republic* and the *Phaedrus.* And pre-
because the venture was one of engaging Greek, preem-
ly Platonic, thought, of broaching a certain *Wiederholung*
ese Platonic texts, the discussion could not avoid touching
.e Heideggerian *Wiederholung* and on other pertinent mo-
s in Heidegger's thought. Our common engagement with
Heideggerian moments was furthered by an event that I
describe below, a public debate in which what Derrida,
ing to Heidegger, called the question of the question came
put in question. The principal traces of this event—though
he only ones—are to be found in Derrida's text *Of Spirit:*
gger and the Question.

hile thus circulating through these other sites, our discus-
etained as its primary locus that defined by the χώρα, which
hus, in this sense, the first and last word of our dialogue. It
his primary site that I will eventually circle back in order to
nt and extend that discussion, yet not before taking up the
events, and questions that pertain to the relevant moments
eidegger's thought and to Derrida's engagement with such
nic dialogues as the *Republic* and the *Phaedrus.*

goes almost without saying that it is not a matter of *present-*
rtain facets of Derrida's work, not a matter of *presentation.*
o one has more thoroughly put in question the concept of
nce: not only has Derrida shown that presence as such is
y implicated in the very constitution of metaphysics but also
s unmasked the dream of full presence to intuition and to
xtent has undermined the classical ideal of presentation.

errida, "Comme si c'était possible," 510; English version in *Questioning Derrida,*

3

Last Words:
Generosity and Reserve

Derrida neither claimed nor advocated the last word. Responding,
in *Revue Internationale de Philosophie*, to a series of discussions of his
work, he begins: "Despite the delay of what begins here, this won't,
as one might suspect, be about the last word. A reader must, above
all, not expect any last word. It is excluded, nearly impossible, that
for my part I would dare to lay claim to one. It would even be necessary, another protocol of the contract, *not* to lay claim to one or
expect one." Yet the title of Derrida's response, "As if it were possible, 'within such limits' . . . ," alludes to the last word, to the final
say that—if it were possible within these limits—the author would
have on the issues raised by those discussing his work, to the last
word that—if it were possible—would settle these issues once and
for all. The title hints indeed at the claim to the last word, yet only
in order to undermine it, only in order to pose—without thereby
claiming the last word—the impossibility of the last word. In place
of this claim, Derrida deploys a writing that reinforces this impossibility, a writing oriented "toward an irreducible modality of 'perhaps,'"
which "would make any authority of the '*last word*' tremble."[1]

1. This issue of *Revue Internationale de Philosophie* (vol. 53, no. 3 [1998]) was organized
by the editor Michel Meyer and included seven essays plus Derrida's response, each

The last words between us come from this context; or, more accurately, the last words addressed to one another in writing and in a public forum occurred in this exchange in *Revue Internationale de Philosophie.* They were not the last words we spoke to one another: those came much later, after he became ill, not long before his death. Even then—as always—it was, in part, about words that we spoke, about a lecture that was soon to appear in English, a lecture that, some months earlier, he had presented at the commemoration, in Heidelberg, of the first anniversary of the death of our friend Hans-Georg Gadamer. The *Stimmung* to which this lecture attests, an ageless melancholy, was no less memorable than its title "Uninterrupted Dialogue."[2]

There has perhaps been no one more acutely aware than he of the extreme precariousness of dialogue, of the manifold of conditions that can so readily come to interrupt it, not only blocking the way ahead but even, all too often, doubling back over what seemed to have been achieved, condemning it to oblivion. This is perhaps why he cherished dialogue as he did, holding back entirely in situations where he knew it was impossible, venturing it whenever there was a glimmer of hope that it might, for a time, go uninterrupted, or, for that matter, that it might go at all, since dialogue can go uninterrupted only by accommodating, indeed thriving on, the possibility of a certain kind of interruption. Because, cherishing it as he did, he was also wary of its pitfalls, dialogue with him was demanding. His unlimited generosity did not result in sheer overflowing of abundance; he seldom simply gave with wide-open arms. It was rather as if, very often, he would have liked to cover his head while making his offering,

published in the original language. Not insignificantly, the title of Derrida's response mixes French and English ("Comme si c'était possible, «within such limits»"), further compounding the question of the last word. Three years later the seven essays plus Derrida's response were published as a book, *Questioning Derrida: With his replies on philosophy,* ed. Michel Meyer (Aldershot: Ashgate, 2001). In the book format all the essays as well as Derrida's response appear in English. The passage cited is from pages 497f. (French) and 96f. (English).

2. Jacques Derrida, "Uninterrupted Dialogue: Between Two Infinities, the Poem," *Research in Phenomenology* 34 (2004): 3–19.

as Socrates once did. Generosity, then, limited by reserve but as if rendered all t

The last words he addressed to me in dialogue, with the dialogue that we h from the early 1980s on. The dialogue a dialogue, with the Platonic dialogue in *Revue Internationale de Philosophie* to he generously mentions "our ongoing di which, for years, has meant so much to m dialogue on this dialogue, deploying in were his last words in the dialogue. Ev ruption is powerless to stem the tide of in a certain way the dialogue will, even on, will survive as these words are bor alters everything.

Now, after his death, we have heard— a sense—his last words. At the cemetery tober 12, 2004, he spoke through the voic to his friends, to those present of cours He thanked them for having come and friendship. He asked them not to weer said: "I bless you. I love you. I am smilin be."[4]

>>><<<

Our dialogue concerned chiefly the *Ti* the χώρα. Yet, as Derrida insists in his discussion necessarily exceeds the singl has "never found a concept that can be

3. "... dans le dialogue que nous poursuivons e années autour de ce texte de Platon..." (Derrida, "C *Internationale de Philosophie,* 522). My essay "Daydrea book *Platonic Legacies* (State University of New Yo written shortly after I completed *Chorology,* my bool which I will refer below); thus the essay makes use book.

4. "Je vous bénis. Je vous aime. Je vous souris, où

Any pretense of *presenting* Derrida's work would not only run aground on his deconstruction of presence but also—more significantly, it seems to me—would deprive his thought of the force of questioning that animates it, that gives it its soul, or— in a word that Derrida rigorously interrogates—that gives it its spirit. In the course of the interrogation, Derrida says—in a saying that he insists is neither a figure nor a metaphor—that it is spirit that inflames. Here, more extendedly, is what he says, or rather asks, as a question of how to translate Heidegger's evocation "Der Geist ist Flamme": "How to translate? Spirit is what inflames? Rather, what inflames *itself,* setting *itself* on fire, setting fire to *itself*? Spirit is flame. A flame which inflames, or which inflames *itself*: both at once, the one and the other, the one the other. *Con*flagration of the two in the very con*flagration*."[6] It is this conflagration, it seems, that Derrida is intent on furthering. Is it not this conflagration that we too should further, even if in engaging Derrida's texts, even if in putting in question certain directions taken in his texts? For fire, as we know, not only consumes and destroys but also separates and purifies. And, as the fire of heaven, even as we imitate it while shielding our eyes from it, it gives life; it brings forth all things and lets them be seen, lets manifestation occur. What could, then, more suitably be called by the name *good*—or at least declared the progeny of the good—in the discourse that both founds metaphysics and, set at the limit, exceeds it.

It is imperative, then, to be attentive to the force of Derrida's questioning, to the force of his thought, indeed even to the force with which he differentiates thought from questioning. In this regard, *force* does not refer to sheer undifferentiated persistence, to a stubborn adherence to a question even at the cost of failing to put the question in question, to say nothing of suspending strategically the authority of questioning as such. Rather, the force of

6. Derrida, *De l'esprit: Heidegger et la question* (Paris: Galilée, 1987), 133. Translated by Geoffrey Bennington and Rachel Bowlby as *Of Spirit: Heidegger and the Question* (Chicago: University of Chicago Press, 1989), 84. Further references will be indicated in the text by *S*, followed by page numbers in the French and English editions, respectively.

questioning such as one observes it in Derrida—but also, equally in Heidegger—includes knowing precisely when and how to take distance from a question, to give it up, to give up on it, and to aim elsewhere, to evoke even what may resist being captured in a question, as a question.

The force of questioning also involves the capacity to hearken to what exceeds the question, to what exceeds it in the direction of anteriority. What is required is engagement with what is anterior to the question, engagement in the sense of giving, in advance, a pledge (*le gage* of *engager*).

My aim in what follows is to show how the force of Derrida's questioning is deployed at each of the three sites to which I referred above. Though, to be sure, the three sites occupy different locations in the topography of Derrida's thought and each has therefore its own configuration of themes and questions, there are, as already suggested, subterranean passages that connect them. Much will depend on discovering these passages and thus on opening or extending communication between these sites, perhaps even in ways that Jacques Derrida never quite envisioned. It would not be incorrect to say that at all three sites what, in the end, is at stake is the very possibility and character of philosophical thought. Yet the sites are quite diverse, and each involves different parameters assembled in different ways; only through attentiveness to the uniqueness of each site can something be gained as regards the general, overarching question of philosophy as such.

Let me stress once more that it is not a matter simply—or not so simply—of presentation. For these are precisely sites where—even now, after the death of Jacques Derrida—much, perhaps almost everything, remains inconclusive, open to questioning, perhaps even in need of a certain retreat from the question. They are open sites where thinking can be deployed today, submitting to all that Jacques Derrida's enormous generosity has given us, while also, precisely in his spirit, hoping to ignite flames that will separate what would otherwise remain indistinct, that will purify—like the refiner's fire—what would otherwise remain contaminated, and that will illuminate and enliven what otherwise would remain exposed to the threat of obscurity and death.

Each of the three sites is linked to a particular text by Derrida. The first site is that of Derrida's engagement with Heidegger, specifically as it is ventured in *Of Spirit: Heidegger and the Question*. Here the theme is precisely that of the question, of what Derrida sometimes calls the privilege of the question or even the question of the question. Needless to say, this theme is not easily separated from any of the others that Derrida explicitly identifies in this text; yet among these other themes, the one that will prove most consequential is the question of essence and of the contamination of essence.

The second site is more difficult to describe, in part because of the richness and complexity of the text "Plato's Pharmacy" to which it is linked. For now, let it suffice to say that the central concern is the relation—and there is none more subtle and more complex—between the withdrawal of the good and the advent of the dialectic supplement, its advent along with a host of other contaminating supplements following in its train. Everything will prove to depend on how this relation is finally to be determined— that is, on whether there remains some prospect of the good or whether all are set entirely adrift amidst supplements. In a sense this comes down to deciding whether it is the good that rules or whether it is the *pharmakon*. In order to animate this question at the limit of "Plato's Pharmacy," it will be imperative to put in play, somewhat independently, both the dialogue to which Derrida's provocative text is largely addressed, namely, the *Phaedrus*, as well as others, such as the *Republic* and the *Phaedo*, that remain somewhat marginal to it.

The third site is best designated by the word—if it be a word— χώρα. This, too, is the title of the relevant text. The χώρα has to do with the very possibility of exteriority, hence with the possibility of sites, of multiple sites where one and the same thought can be envisaged. It is not only in this respect that the third site communicates with the others; it does so also by the way in which it disfigures what would be—and in a certain way remains—one and the same, that which eventually comes to be designated by the word *essence.*

>>><<<

The genesis of Derrida's *Of Spirit* is not insignificant. The book has links to the series of pieces that Derrida entitled "Geschlecht"; he refers to this designation as "that frighteningly polysemic and practically untranslatable word (race, lineage, stock, generation, sex)" (*S* 22/7). To the first piece thus entitled, Derrida added the subtitle "sexual difference, ontological difference." First published in 1983, this essay follows certain traces in Heidegger's 1928 course *Metaphysische Anfangsgründe der Logik* that lead from the sexual neutrality of Dasein to its originary dispersion (*Zerstreuung*) and then to its dispersion into sexual difference.[7] The second "Geschlecht" adds the subtitle "Heidegger's Hand"; again following certain traces in Heidegger's texts—in such texts as *Was heisst Denken?*—Derrida's focus is on the hand as the monstrous sign proper to man.[8] At the conference in Chicago at which Derrida read the English text of "Geschlecht II," he also distributed to the other participants a fragment called "Geschlecht III," which has never been published.[9] Though still another text, "Geschlecht IV," was delivered in 1989, two years after *Of Spirit,* and was

7. Derrida, "Geschlecht, différence sexuelle, différence ontologique," in *Heidegger* (Paris: Cahiers de l'Herne, 1983). English version: "Geschlecht, sexual difference, ontological difference," *Research in Phenomenology* 13 (1983): 65–83.

8. Derrida, "Geschlecht II: La Main de Heidegger," in *Psyché* (Paris: Galilée, 1987). Translated by John P. Leavey, Jr., as "Geschlecht II: Heidegger's Hand," in *Deconstruction and Philosophy: The Texts of Jacques Derrida,* ed. John Sallis (Chicago: University of Chicago Press, 1987).

9. The conference, entitled "Deconstruction and Philosophy: The Texts of Jacques Derrida," was held at Loyola University of Chicago on March 22–23, 1985. David Krell, who was a participant in the conference in Chicago and who subsequently corresponded with Derrida regarding "Geschlecht III," has written two papers that situate "Geschlecht III," describe its contents, and outline the subsequent correspondence: (1) "One, Two, Four—Yet Where Is the Third? A Note on Derrida's *Geschlecht* Series," (*Epoché* 10, no. 2 [Spring 2006]: 341–57); and (2) "Marginalia to *Geschlecht III:* Derrida on Heidegger on Trakl" (to be published in *New Contemporary Review*).

subsequently published,[10] the "Geschlecht" series remains incomplete. This series shares several motifs with *Of Spirit*, among them a concern with Heidegger's interpretation of Trakl's poetry.

Derrida's first public announcement of the project that led to *Of Spirit* was given at a conference organized by David Krell at the University of Essex in 1986. In the penultimate version of the project as presented at the Essex conference, Derrida already introduced the four guiding threads that were to be reiterated near the outset of *Of Spirit*, though it is only in the book itself (delivered as a lecture at a conference in Paris in 1987) that spirit is identified as what weaves and knots together the four threads.

At the first of the three sites outlined above, what is primarily contested is the question—that is, the authority of the question as such. To be sure, this is only one of the four guiding threads running through *Of Spirit*. Yet the subtitle *Heidegger and the Question* suggests that this first guiding thread has a certain precedence, as is suggested also by the directness with which it comes to be knotted together with the other three threads. The connection will prove most direct in the case of the second guiding thread, which Derrida introduces through the exemplary statement "The essence of technology is nothing technological" or, more literally, "The essence of technology is not technology [*l'essence de la technique n'est pas technique*]" (*S* 26/10). Derrida broaches the intertwining immediately: this statement, he says, "maintains the possibility of thought that questions, which is always thought of the essence, protected from any original and essential contamination by technology" (*S* 26/10). Thus it is evident that what is at issue here is not primarily technology but rather essence itself, which in turn is precisely that at which thought that questions is directed, that toward which thought determined as questioning is oriented. Essence itself, essence as such—and essence is

10. Though the designation *Geschlecht* remains, it is reduced to a parenthesized addition to the subtitle. Thus the full title of the piece is "Heidegger's Ear: Philopolemology (*Geschlecht* IV)." Translated by John P. Leavey, Jr., in *Reading Heidegger: Commemorations*, ed. John Sallis (Bloomington: Indiana University Press, 1993), 163–218.

precisely the *itself,* the *as such*—is what is put in question in the philosophical question as such.

There are connections also with the other guiding threads, those concerning animality and epochality. But they are more remote and can for the most part be left aside as we turn to the contesting of the question.

In this contestation what is to be taken up is designated by Derrida as the question of the question. Yet clearly it is not a matter of simply repeating the interrogative in the empty form "Why the why?" Rather, it is a matter of putting in question something about the question as such and of proceeding in a way that would not simply reaffirm at another level what is being put into question. What is it, then, about the question that is to be put into question? It is, in Derrida's words, "the apparently absolute and long unquestioned privilege of the *Fragen*" (*S* 24/9). What is the privilege accorded to questioning? The privilege consists in questioning being taken as constituting thinking as such in the purest, most fundamental, most anterior form. Thinking—so it is maintained—is fundamentally questioning. To be sure, Heidegger differentiates various modes of questioning and analyzes its mere reflexive repetition; but none of these analyses alter in the least the privileging of the question. Thinking is most thoroughly itself precisely when it poses and pursues the question. Thinking is essentially questioning.

Or rather, such is the position that Derrida ascribes to Heidegger. Indeed at the Essex conference Derrida was utterly direct. There he said: "The question is privileged everywhere by Heidegger as the mode of thinking."[11] Yet less than a year later, in *Of Spirit,* Derrida is more circumspect, saying of Heidegger: "But,

11. An outline of Derrida's lecture from the Essex conference was prepared by David Krell, approved by Derrida, and published as "On Reading Heidegger: An Outline of Remarks to the Essex Colloquium," in *Research in Phenomenology* 17 (1987): 171–74. The sentence cited occurs also in the outline (171). A transcript of the official discussion following Derrida's lecture is appended to the outline. There were additional discussions that are not recorded here, such as the one with Françoise Dastur to which Derrida later refers in *Of Spirit* and which I will discuss below.

it seems to me, he *almost* never stopped identifying what is highest and best in thought with the question" (*S* 24f. /9). Derrida's cautiousness is marked in the sentence, the word *almost* being italicized. This cautiousness, this opening to an exceptional instance in which Heidegger might indeed not have privileged the question, is linked to what happened during the Essex conference, in the discussion following Derrida's lecture. As we will confirm, this *almost* that comes to qualify Heidegger's privileging of the question is by no means the only trace of this discussion to be found in *Of Spirit.* The consequences of Derrida's cautious opening will prove to be almost—if not entirely—unlimited.

Derrida refers to the dictum with which Heidegger concludes "The Question concerning Technology": that questioning is the piety of thought. Even in this dictum, which seems to affirm without qualification the absolute privileging of questioning, Derrida detects already a limit that would limit—and hence revoke—the apparent absoluteness. For he asks whether this decision—that questioning is the piety of thought—is itself a questioning or whether it is a sheltering of the question anterior to the question itself. Still more striking is the passage, cited by Derrida in a note, in which Heidegger explains that in the dictum "Questioning is the piety of thought" the word *pious* is to be taken to mean— these are Heidegger's words—"*fügsam dem Walten und Verwahren der Wahrheit* [yielding, obedient, responsive—Derrida translates *fügsam* as docile—to the holding sway and securing of truth]" (*S* 25 n. 1/117 n. 4). These words could hardly be taken otherwise than as referring to an anteriority to which questioning would—at its limit, as its limit—submit.

And yet, while pushing toward such anteriority and even, with this citation, pushing Heidegger in this direction, Derrida continues to take Heidegger as—almost always—having privileged the question. What concerns Derrida, then, is how—by what means—this privileging of the question was protected, sheltered, how it remained *à l'abri* (under shelter). This is the point where the curtain opens and spirit makes its entry on the scene: "Now *Geist,* as I will attempt to show, is perhaps the name Heidegger gives, beyond any other name, to this unquestioned possibility of the question" (*S* 25f. /10).

Derrida undertakes to show this in his interpretation of Heidegger's 1935 lecture course *Einführung in die Metaphysik*. If the absolute privilege of the question is granted, then there can be nothing that precedes the question, nothing anterior that would dictate it. Whatever comes before, whatever, as its introduction, leads to questioning, must be—in Derrida's words—"an already questioning fore-coming of the question (*ein fragendes Vorangehen*), a pre-questioning [*un pré-questionnement*], *ein Vor-fragen*" (*S* 69/43). Thus the question in its absoluteness, its freedom, does not have to be introduced—cannot be introduced—"from anything other than an *already* questioning conduction: *and*"— Derrida writes, now italicizing—"*this is spirit itself*" (*S* 70/43). In this way, spirit, the freedom of spirit, would shelter the privilege of the question; indeed spirit would be the very assertion of this privilege.

The security of this privilege would, to the end, be entrusted to spirit. Almost always—recalling the exception for which Derrida has discreetly left room—the question of the question will be—will prove to have been—interwoven with the story of how Heidegger attempted to save spirit, to distill the spirit of spirit, to distinguish the "true" spirit and to set it apart from its subjective, metaphysical double.

In the course of this story and yet somewhat apart from it, Derrida returns, in the penultimate chapter of *Of Spirit*, to the question of the question. Again he pushes toward an anteriority that would limit, rather than simply protecting, the privilege of the question. The Heideggerian idiom remains in play, since it is Heidegger's interpretation of Trakl that at this point is primarily under discussion; and yet, the move toward anteriority is not carried out as a move traceable in Heidegger's text; or rather, it is almost never carried out in this way, almost never cast as a reenactment of a move effected by Heidegger himself, almost never attributed to Heidegger himself. Almost never. Never— except in a long footnote composed after the Essex conference and in response to something that happened there. Furthermore, in his indication that *Of Spirit* was first presented at the conference "Heidegger: Questions Ouvertes" (held on March 14, 1987, at the Collège International de Philosophie in Paris), Derrida mentions that "the notes were obviously added later"; hence, we may be assured that, in particular, the long note on Heidegger and the question of the question postdates the composition of the text of *Of Spirit*. Indeed, at least as regards the interpretation of Heidegger's stance regarding the question, the note has little or no resonance in Derrida's text proper.

In the course of discussing Heidegger's interpretation of Trakl, Derrida comes to write about the promise, about the promise offered by speech, the promise that speech holds out in advance of all speaking. Derrida proposes that it is in this opening that the speaking of thinker and of poet cross in their *Gespräch*. Thus playing on the Heideggerian dictum "Die Sprache spricht," Derrida writes: Die Sprache verspricht (Language promises). Then, in a crucial, if still interrogative move, Derrida puts forth this *Versprechen*, this promise of language itself, as what precedes the question and thus limits its privilege. Here is Derrida's formulation: "It remains to find out whether this *Versprechen* is not the promise which, opening every speaking, makes possible the question itself and therefore precedes it without belonging to it: the dissymmetry of an affirmation, of a *yes* before all opposition of *yes* and *no*. The call of Being—every question already responds to it, the promise has already taken place wherever language comes" (*S* 147/94). Here Derrida names—multiply—the anteriority toward which he has been pushing, an anteriority apart from the question, an anteriority that would open every speaking and thus make possible the question, limiting its privilege. The names given here to this anteriority form a curious mix, a mix of the languages, a mix of the Heideggerian idiom with another that has begun to emerge. Among its names are *Versprechen, la promesse, the call of Being* (yet said in French: *l'appel de l'être*), *langage* in distinction from the *parole* that it renders possible, an affirmation in which *yes* would be enacted in advance of any saying of *yes* and *no*. Then, with the multiplicity of names announced, Derrida makes another crucial move: he reduces the entire configuration to its absolute minimum, distilling this abundance of language, this excess, into a mere five words. He begins: "Celui-ci toujours,"—and then continues in italics: "*avant toute question.*" In the translation the sentence—or rather, sentence fragment—reads, "Language always, *before any question*" (*S* 147/94). After these five words, indeed before going on to complete the sentence by bringing everything around to, back to, the promise, Derrida inserts a footnote. The note runs on for several pages, disfiguring the French text, taking over the text and leaving room on each of the following seven pages for only a few lines of what otherwise one would take as the main text. This graphic effect is not insignificant.

At the end of the long note Derrida mentions that it is dedicated to Françoise Dastur, who at the Essex conference reminded him of a certain passage in *Unterwegs zur Sprache*. Indeed all who were there will recall the moment, a moment not without a certain tension. It came almost immediately after Derrida had completed his lecture, in the course of which he had declared, "The question is privileged everywhere by Heidegger as *the* mode of thinking." Dastur insisted that it was otherwise and, to substantiate her disagreement, cited a passage in which indeed Heidegger himself declares just the opposite. The passage occurs in the 1958 essay "Das Wesen der Sprache." Heidegger has just mentioned that every question remains within the *Zusage* (one meaning of the word is *promise*) of that which is put in question. He continues: "Was erfahren wir, wenn wir dies genügend bedenken? Dass das Fragen nicht die eigentliche Gebärde des Denkens ist, sondern—das Hören der Zusage dessen, was in die Frage kommen soll."[12] In the note in *Of Spirit*, Derrida translates the passage, though he leaves the key word *Zusage* untranslated,

---

12. Martin Heidegger, *Unterwegs zur Sprache* (Pfullingen: Günther Neske, 1959), 175. Though Derrida attaches the date 1958 to the essay "Das Wesen der Sprache," the *Hinweise* in *Unterwegs zur Sprache* reports that it was presented in Freiburg as a series of three lectures on December 4,1957; December 18, 1957; and February 7, 1958.

observing that at least three distinct meanings are in play in it: promise, agreement or consent, and originary abandonment to what is given in the promise itself.[13] Letting Derrida's translation slip into English, we can translate the passage thus: "What is our experience when we sufficiently meditate on this? That questioning is not the gesture proper to thinking, but rather—listening to the *Zusage* of what is to come into question" (*S* 148/130; translation modified). In other words, thinking is, most properly, not questioning, but listening to the *Zusage*.

At the moment when he has just cited the crucial passage from Heidegger, Derrida confirms that—as he will put it some years later—the passage makes any authority of the *last word* tremble. In this case it is the question that would have been the last word; that is, with the reference to the question, one would have had the last word. In particular, Heidegger, it seems, prior to 1958, would have taken himself—in referring to the question, in declaring questioning to be the piety of thinking—to have had the last word. But now that authority is shaken: "The question is thus not the last word in language" (*S* 148/130). It is not the last word because it is not the first word, not a word that would already constitute its own anteriority. Rather, before the question there is the wordless *yes*, the engaging of an anteriority unassimilable to the question.

Even before, in the note, Derrida cites the crucial passage from Heidegger, he resumes the push toward such an anteriority, doubling in the note the move that has already commenced in the text proper. As before, he enacts it himself, in terms even more his own than previously, leaving Heidegger aside up to the point where, finally, preparing to cite the passage marshaled by Françoise Dastur, he grants that Heidegger too enacted the move from the question to the anteriority that opens its very possibility. It

13. The range of meanings of *Zusage* and their configuration (as sketched by Derrida) are such that one might regard *Zusage* as analogous to what Hegel calls a speculative word (as with *Aufheben*). Yet in this case the sense of analogy would need to be determined in such a way as to span the difference produced by the deconstruction of the history of metaphysics.

is a matter of what lies before any question, and the note begins
by repeating these words:

> Before any question, then. It is precisely here that the "question of
> the question," which has been dogging us since the beginning of
> this journey, vacillates. It vacillates at this moment when it is no
> longer a question. Not that it withdraws from the infinite legitimacy
> of questioning, but it tips over into the memory of a language, of an
> experience of language "older" than it, always anterior and presup-
> posed, old enough never to have been present in an "experience" or
> a "speech act"—in the usual sense of these words. This moment—
> which is not a moment—is *marked* in Heidegger's text..., in lit-
> eral and extremely explicit fashion in "Das Wesen der Sprache." (*S*
> 147/129)

As Derrida continues, in the note, to reformulate again and
again this move from the question to its anteriority, his language
resumes mixing with the Heideggerian idiom. He writes, for
instance, very succinctly: "Language is *already* there, in advance
(*im voraus*) at the moment at which any question can arise about
it. In this it exceeds the question" (*S* 148/129). He expresses this
already, this excess, as the pre-interrogative, pre-originary *yes*, as
the assent or consent, the abandonment, all of which are gathered
in the Heideggerian *Zusage*. Derrida mentions also Heidegger's
reference in "Das Wesen der Sprache" to the earlier dictum that
questioning is the piety of thought, and he notes how Heidegger
now situates the dictum entirely within the orbit of the *Zusage*.
Indeed Derrida grants that the entire lecture "Das Wesen der
Sprache" is situated within this orbit. Still more decisively, Derrida grants that the thought of an anteriority more proper to
thought than any question opened by it must have an unlimitable
effect on the entirety of Heidegger's path of thought up to the
point where, in "Das Wesen der Sprache," this thought of anteriority first appears. The regression achieved in the 1958 text, the
regression from the question to its anteriority, changes everything
that preceded; it "transforms or deforms (as you like) the whole
landscape" (*S* 149/131). It effects a retrospective upheaval at every

site on that landscape where the privilege of the question was decisive, now unraveling those results, setting them in a new light.

And yet, having granted this inevitable upheaval, Derrida then draws a limit and takes a stand with regard to this limit. While granting that the effect of what comes to pass in the 1958 text cannot but spread back across the expanse of Heidegger's previous thought, he refuses to legitimate a recommencement, that is, a reconstitution of Heidegger's entire path of thought within the orbit of the *Zusage*. Derrida could not be more insistent: it cannot be a matter of now beginning with thought's adherence to anteriority, of taking what appeared only in 1958 as having somehow, imperceptibly, guided Heidegger's thought all along, and thus now of tracing a very different path from the one that otherwise— aside from what appears in 1958—Heidegger's thought would have been taken to follow. To demand such a recommencement would be, Derrida insists, to fail to understand the irreversible necessity of a path that breaks through to what could not have been seen otherwise, otherwise than by following the narrow and perilous path leading from *Being and Time* to "Das Wesen der Sprache." When the retreat to anteriority is finally carried out, it is, says Derrida, "already too late, always too late" (*S* 150/132): the privilege of the question has already been operative and has determined Heidegger's thought for more than three decades. This operation, this determination, cannot, Derrida insists, be undone retrospectively. At most, retrospection can now discern certain strata along Heidegger's way that were until now scarcely visible, certain markers and signs that can now be recognized as pointing ahead—however unsystematically, even incoherently—to the retreat from the question. Derrida lists several such markers and signs: everything in *Being and Time* that concerns the call, most notably, of conscience; certain aspects of the analysis of resoluteness; the discussion of the calling and the promise in *Was heisst Denken?*

From the outset one of the motifs that Derrida pursues in *Of Spirit* is that of avoiding (*éviter, vermeiden*). He details, for instance, how in *Being and Time* Heidegger avoids the word *spirit* because of its subjective, metaphysical legacy, but also how by setting it in quotation marks he avoids it while also using it, as if thereby designating the true spirit of spirit. Something very similar occurs again when the animal, though having no world, is yet said to be *weltarm,* not *weltlos* like a stone. Also, it is well known that in later works Heidegger uses a cross or an × to cross out strategically certain words such as *Being,* thus letting them remain while avoiding a certain legacy that otherwise comes with them.

These strategies of avoidance form the background for what is perhaps the most remarkable of all the passages in the long note that interrupts Derrida's text. The passage marks a pause in the explanation to which otherwise the note is devoted. Indeed Derrida marks it as a pause, saying at the outset: "Pause for a moment"—and then at the end: "End of pause." The pause is made in order, as he says, to dream—to dream of what Heidegger's texts would look like if all the inscriptive devices for avoidance were applied to them. At the high point of the dream, the dreamer would "cross through without a cross all the question marks when it's a question of language"—that is, the dream would become that of a thorough recommencement inscribed in Heidegger's texts. Here is Derrida's analysis of the dream: "One can imagine the surface of a text given over to the gnawing, ruminant, and silent voracity of such an animal-machine and its implacable 'logic.' This would not only be simply 'without spirit,' but a figure of evil. The perverse reading of Heidegger" (*S* 153/134).

And yet—now interrupting this long interruption—we cannot but wonder about this dream. Can the project of recommencement produce only a bad dream, a spiritless, perverse, even evil reading of Heidegger? Is the retreat that the passage from "Das Wesen der Sprache" marks only a late result to which Heidegger's path leads, an outcome that could be legitimated for all preceding it only at the cost of effacing or otherwise altering—hence avoiding—so much along that path that only a perverse reading could be produced? In this case all that Derrida writes in *Of Spirit* about the Heideggerian privileging of the question would remain intact except for this late phase of Heidegger's thought. Or, on the contrary, does the passage only state more explicitly something already affirmed earlier, perhaps even from the outset? Is there to be found along Heidegger's way something more than mere markers and signs that, at most, intimate—yet decisively do *not* effect—the limiting of the privilege of the question? Are passages to be found along that way, perhaps all along that way, that effect already the retreat to anteriority? In this case the possibility of a recommencement would be reopened, the possibility of rereading Heidegger from the beginning by beginning with the retreat from the question. Then it would be a matter, not of condemning such a rereading as perverse, but rather only of measuring the extent to which artifices of avoidance would still be required.

Such passages are indeed to be found, earlier passages that serve already to open Heidegger's way to the question of the question and to the retreat of thinking from the question.

Nearly ten years before "Das Wesen der Sprache," in the 1949 *Einleitung* that Heidegger added to the 1929 lecture "Was Ist Metaphysik?", there is a passage addressed to the pre-originary adherence of thought to that which is to be thought, its adherence to *die Sache des Denkens*. Most remarkably, this passage also refers such adherence of thought back to *Being and Time*. The passage reads: "The thinking attempted in *Being and Time* (1927) sets out on the way to preparing the . . . overcoming of metaphysics. But that which brings such thinking onto its way can only be that which is itself to be thought [*das zu Denkende selbst*]."[14] In a note added to the passage, Heidegger writes the phrase "Was *heisst* Denken?", italicizing the word *heisst,* thus connecting thought's adherence to its *Sache* with the calling, the promise, the *Zusage*.

In *Being and Time* itself, the question as such plays an important role—as Derrida has emphasized—in establishing the point of departure. One must acknowledge the significance that

14. Heidegger, Einleitung zu "Was ist Metaphysik?" in vol. 9 of *Gesamtausgabe* (Frankfurt A.M.: Vittorio Klostermann, 1976), 368.

Dasein's relation to the question has for Heidegger's project, since it is precisely questioning that is taken, along with *Jemeinigkeit* (mineness), to define the comportment characteristic of Dasein. Nonetheless, as, beyond the mere beginning, the concrete structures of Dasein's disclosedness (*Erschlossenheit*) come to be unfolded, there are developments that run counter to the privilege of the question. An especially portentous instance is the analysis in which *Rede* is displayed as a component of Dasein's disclosedness along with *Befindlichkeit* and *Verstehen*. *Rede* constitutes the existential-ontological foundation of speech (*Sprache*) and is identified by Heidegger as *die Artikulation der Verständlichkeit*. In effect what Heidegger's analysis shows is that before there is speech there is always already an articulation of the *Verständlichkeit* that belongs to Dasein's disclosedness. Before any question that Dasein may pose about its Being, there is a prearticulation of sense that must already have been assumed. Before any question this prearticulation must already have been attended to, its promise heard. In the word *Rede*, which is Heidegger's translation of λόγος, one can hear already *Zusage*, the promise; here already there is the promise of the promise.

The bearing of these Heideggerian texts on the question of the question could hardly be more decisive. Indeed, at the other two sites, to which we will soon turn, we will find it equally imperative to bring to bear on the Derridean *Gespräch* certain other texts from outside the immediate environs of the *Gespräch*. In every case the concern is to show how—extending Derrida's metaphor—the threads of these very different fabrics come to be knotted together, even if at the cost of stretching, overlapping, tearing, or ripping apart the fabrics.

>>><<<

But where is the passage to be found that will lead from the site of the question of the question to the site linked to Derrida's text "Plato's Pharmacy"? Once questioning is allowed to slip into its proper questionableness, how does it serve to open—even if subterraneously—a way to the site of the *pharmakon*?

The passage in "Das Wesen der Sprache" leads on to the essential. One has only to read on beyond the sentences cited in Essex by Françoise Dastur and then in the long footnote by Derrida. As Heidegger continues in the passage, he connects the question of the question to the question of essence, thus knotting together the first two of the guiding threads enumerated in *Of Spirit*. Heidegger refers to the determination of essence as ground, that is, as the *radix* that ultimately supports, or, to say it in Greek, the ἀρχή. Then he writes: "The thinking that thinks toward essence as so determined is in its ground a questioning."[15] The consequence is compelling: to take up the question of the question, to contest the identification of thinking with questioning—as both Heidegger and Derrida do, seemingly without limit—is to put in question also the very determination of essence that has prevailed throughout the history of metaphysics. Little wonder, then, that, from 1930 on, as one sees most directly in his text *Vom Wesen der Wahrheit*,[16] Heidegger never ceased being engaged in a redetermination of essence.[17] And yet, as he also never ceased stressing, such an engagement must be paired with the deconstruction of Greek metaphysics; what this requires, above all, is an analysis—a deconstruction, if you will—of the Platonic determination that came to be handed down as the determination of *essentia*. This determination is nothing less than the fundamental determination made operative through Platonic thought, a determination so fundamental that it determined even the very sense of fundamental that would prevail throughout the history of metaphysics. It is the determination of what things are, of their being, as εἶδος or ἰδέα.

15. Heidegger, *Unterwegs zur Sprache*, 175.

16. Heidegger, *Vom Wesen der Wahrheit*, in vol. 9 of *Gesamtausgabe* (Frankfurt A.M.: Vittorio Klostermann, 1976).

17. On Heidegger's redetermination of essence, see my account in *Double Truth* (Albany: State University of New York Press, 1995), chap. 6. During the discussion of Derrida's lecture at the Essex conference, I raised some questions by referring to this redetermination as carried out in *Vom Wesen der Wahrheit*. A transcript of this exchange is included in the appendix to Derrida's "Reading Heidegger," 180.

Thus, as questioning becomes properly questionable, that to which it is oriented as such, essence as such, becomes questionable in its most basic determination. What is called for is a critical (or, if you will, deconstructive) return to the originary determination of being as it came about in the Platonic texts. It is this determination that comes to be exposed to Plato's pharmacy.

>>><<<

It may seem that "Plato's Pharmacy" is rather remote from this task. In this text Derrida's concern seems to be primarily with writing and with the apparent devaluation of writing in relation to speech. For the most part Derrida's text is devoted to a close interpretation of the final pages of the *Phaedrus,* in which writing is indisputably the primary theme. Thus it would appear that "Plato's Pharmacy" is dedicated principally to demonstrating and interrogating Plato's so-called phonocentrism and that it is only quite obliquely that it bears on the question of the determination or deconstruction of essence. And yet, what is perhaps most immediately striking about the *pharmakon* is its resistance to being essentially anything, its withdrawal from essential determination. "Plato's Pharmacy" thus approaches the question of essence obliquely. It is oriented less toward essence as such than toward a certain resistance to essence, toward essential withdrawal, which will prove to be both withdrawal from essence and a correlative withdrawal of essence as such. Here, then, one can begin to see how "Plato's Pharmacy" carries out a critical or deconstructive interrogation of essence, that is, one that seeks to mark the limits of this determination. If, as I will propose, an oblique reading is, in turn, brought to bear on this oblique approach, a reading that confronts "Plato's Pharmacy" with certain Platonic texts, inaugurating, beyond "Plato's Pharmacy" itself, still another *Gespräch* between it and these Platonic texts, a *Gespräch* that brings them in from the outside to the inside to which they already belong, then one may well expect that a different spacing will begin to take place—perhaps even that a flame will flare up, a flame intense enough to set apart while also reducing to ashes.

In "Plato's Pharmacy" withdrawal is in play everywhere, not least of all in the *pharmakon* as such, or rather, in the very withdrawal of its *as such*, in its very withdrawal from the *as such*. There is no *pharmakon* as such; it has no essence that would render it substantial. It harbors within itself a complicity of contrary values: thus it can present itself as a poison yet turn out to be a cure, which in turn cannot but be also harmful, something artificial that acts counter to natural life. Derrida writes of it: "The 'essence' [quotation marks around this word serve to withdraw it] of the *pharmakon* lies in the way in which, having no stable essence [here the withdrawal is explicit], no proper character, it is not, in any sense of the word (metaphysical, physical, chemical, alchemical), a *substance*." Then Derrida adds, most tellingly: "The *pharmakon* has no ideal identity; it is aneidetic" (*D* 144/125f.). In other words, the *pharmakon* withdraws from essential, ideal determination, from determination through—determination as—an εἶδος.

Derrida proposes a decisive further step. He declares that the *pharmakon* not only resists appropriation to an εἶδος but also that it is prior to the very opposition between the eidetic and the particular, that it is the prior medium from which this opposition first emerges. In Derrida's words: "It is rather the anterior medium in which differentiation in general is produced, along with the opposition between the *eidos* and its other" (*D* 144/126). The massive ambiguity of the reference to production makes it difficult to determine precisely how this declaration is to be taken. Is the *pharmakon* like the example of the three fingers given in the *Republic*, that is, such that it provokes thought and leads one to draw the distinction between one and many, to set the one beings, the εἴδη, over against the indistinct mixture? Is it, as in this example, a matter of a distinction that merely affirms and makes manifest an anterior differentiation, an opposition already in force? Or is it rather that the opposition is in no way anterior to the *pharmakon* but rather first arises, first comes into force, only beginning with the *pharmakon*, only from the *pharmakon*? Needless to say, there is much in the dialogues that would strongly resist the second alternative, at least its unconditional assertion.

That is, there is much—more than could ever be set aside—that precludes making the one beings, the εἴδη, finally dependent on their separation from a prior mixture. Even in the *Timaeus* they are apart from the mixture wrought in the receptacle, and in a sense the entire question of the receptacle is inseparable from this apartness.

In the *pharmakon,* according to Derrida, there is unlimited, absolute passage between opposites: something replaces something else, thereby takes on the shape of its opposite, hence comes to be opposed to itself, that is, it passes into its opposite. This would be, as Derrida notes, the mediating movement of dialectic (in Hegel's sense), were the passage not indefinitely prevented by mimicry and doubling. The interruption of this passage and the passage beyond it to the stabilized opposition between the εἶδος and the sensible thing Derrida takes to be a decision on the part of Plato. He writes: "On the one hand Plato decides [*avance la décision*] in favor of a logic that does not tolerate such passages between opposing senses of the same word. . . . And yet, on the other hand, the *pharmakon* . . . constitutes the original medium of that decision, the element that precedes it, comprehends it, goes beyond it, and can never be reduced to it" (*D* iiif. /99). And yet, one might respond that, if this move is a decision, it is neither arbitrary nor unmotivated, as the example of the three fingers shows clearly. Furthermore, it remains to be shown how the pharmacological swirl of opposites fails to be comprehended by the fundamental Platonic opposition, that is, how there is a remainder that compromises the exclusiveness of this opposition. Are the opposites as well as the ones with which dialectic would stabilize their swirl drawn finally from their bottomless fund (*fonds sans fond*)? Does everything that is anything, everything that imposes or submits to essential determination, recline finally on such a store of deep background (*réserve d'arrière-fond*) constituted by the *pharmakon,* by what is not anything in itself? Does everything come down to the pharmacy?

In any case it is evident that in what he says about the *pharmakon* he is venturing to think it as a third kind, as a τρίτον γένος in the idiom of the *Timaeus*. Though this goes unmentioned, it is presumably the reason that he links the *pharmakon* to another third kind, *ein Drittes*, as Kant called it, the transcendental imagination: "this medium is *analogous* to the one that will, subsequent to and according to the decision of philosophy, be reserved for transcendental imagination, that 'art hidden in the depths of the soul,' which belongs neither simply to the sensible nor simply to the intelligible" (*D* 144/126). There are other significant indications that in the thinking and rethinking of the *pharmakon* there is already broached, however tentatively, what will be thought systematically—in an exorbitant sense of course—as the χώρα. One indication is given by Derrida's remark that the *pharmakon* makes one *stray*, as the writing, the speech of Lysias, brought along by Phaedrus, leads Socrates to stray beyond his usual practices and habits, to stray outside the city (see *D* 79/70). What will eventually be named χώρα is closely linked, in advance, to what Timaeus calls the *errant* cause, the word πλανωμένη carrying the double sense of *wandering* and of *erring*. A second indication is provided by Derrida's statement: "The *pharmakon* is that which, always springing up from without, acting like the outside itself, will never have any definable virtue of its own" (*D* 115/102). In the *Timaeus* the χώρα will prove to be—let me say for now, already crossing out, erasing, almost everything in the saying—the outside itself or, if you will, the very outside of being itself. Indeed, toward the end of "Plato's Pharmacy," Derrida cites virtually the entire passage on the χώρα from the *Timaeus*, having said that "It is a matrix, womb [*matrice*], receptacle that is never and nowhere offered up in the form of presence, or in the presence of form, since both of these already presuppose an inscription within the mother" (*D* 184/160). Immediately following the citation, Derrida promises: "We will go into that elsewhere." That "elsewhere" is of course the text entitled *Khôra*.

Yet there is another direction that, aside from the minimal comments in "Plato's Pharmacy," Derrida never took up. For there is another dialogue, the *Phaedo,* in which the role of the *pharmakon* is comparable in importance to that in the *Phaedrus*.

Indeed, one could well imagine a companion piece to "Plato's Pharmacy," perhaps even one homonymous with it, yet devoted to the *pharmakon* in the *Phaedo*. In this dialogue the *pharmakon* is in play, quite literally, from beginning to end. The very first sentence refers to the potion that Socrates drank in prison; the word that is so readily translated as *potion* or, even worse, as *poison*, is *pharmakon*, and this is in fact the only word used in the dialogue to refer to this liquid. As soon as one translates the word as *poison* or, in translating, identifies it as *hemlock*, one has interrupted the play of the *pharmakon*. And yet, it continues right up through Socrates' final words instructing Crito that a debt is to be paid, that, as Socrates says, "we owe a cock to Asclepius" (*Phaedo* 118). Socrates—and presumably also his friends there in the prison cell—has recovered from an illness; something medicinal has been effective there at the very scene of death, in the very time leading up to the moment when the poison finally has its effect. Everything depends on how this medicinal effect is understood in relation to the dramatic development within which the λόγοι of the dialogue are contextualized. Does it suffice, as Derrida proposes, to regard the immortality of the soul as the operative antibody, as the means of deliverance that dialectically inverts and in a sense stabilizes the *pharmakon* (see *D* 140/123, 144f. /126)? Does it suffice to call a halt to the dialogue's development at this initial, Orphic-Pythagorean threshold, especially in view of all that undoes the would-be demonstrations of the deathlessness of the soul? Is the recovery for which a cock is owed to Asclepius a recovery from embodiment, from human life itself, or is it rather a recovery in which the arrogance of an impossible, inhuman knowledge finally gives way to a properly Socratic attesting to ignorance?

Such are the questions—and their antecedents—to which such a double of "Plato's Pharmacy" would need to be directed. Yet its effect would be, not to displace and replace Derrida's text, but to complement it in such a way that, subsequently, a productive exchange might become possible.

There is another withdrawal that in certain respects is still more consequential than that of the *pharmakon* "as such"; it is, in any case, decisive in and for "Plato's Pharmacy." Its lines, even those that are barely discernible, need to be traced with utmost care. It is especially on the configuration thus resulting that an oblique reading will eventually be brought to bear.

This withdrawal is linked to dialectic. Indeed, it is precisely in relation to this withdrawal that, according to Derrida, dialectic is determined, that it is released, set under way. What, then, is it that, in withdrawing, sets dialectic under way? Derrida takes it to be, preeminently, that which the *Republic* calls the good (τὸ ἀγαθόν). Drawing on various passages both in the *Republic* and elsewhere, Derrida multiplies the designations, lets them expand into a series. Especially significant in this regard is the passage in the *Republic* (506e) where Socrates forgoes speaking of the good itself and proposes instead to speak of its offspring, of its child (ἔκγονος), the sun. Thus is implied also the designation of the good as the father. Derrida draws out several links that this designation sustains: to the prospect of parricide in the interrogation of father Parmenides carried out in the *Sophist* (see *D* 189f. /164, which cites *Sophist* 241d–42a); to the relation that obtains between λόγος (which is like a living being) and its father, both when, as in living speech, the father is present and when, as in writing, the father is absent, even dead. Derrida also cites (see *D* 185f. /160f.)—without yet developing—the passage in the *Timaeus* where the designation *father* is more thoroughly carried through by way of the addition—along with father and child—of the mother. Proceeding again from the passage in the *Republic* where Socrates forgoes speaking of the good itself, Derrida calls attention to the specifically economic terms that are introduced. When, in face of Socrates' proposal, Glaucon agrees to defer being paid the story of the parent, Socrates responds that, though he wishes he could make the payment, he will for now deliver to Glaucon only the interest. The word τόκος means both offspring and, metaphorically, the interest produced by capital. Thus the series of designations is formed: good, sun, father, capital.

These designate, then, that which, in withdrawing, sets dialectic under way. Beginning in the wake of this withdrawal, dialectic assumes the guise of a supplement: "dialectics supplements and replaces [this hendiadys translates the single word *supplée*] the impossible *noēsis*, the forbidden intuition of the face of the father (good-sun-capital). The withdrawal [*retrait*] of that face both opens and limits the exercise of dialectics" (*D* 193/167).

Above all, it seems, the withdrawal *limits* dialectic, keeps it remote from the truth of beings, irremediably distanced from any showing in which things would show themselves as they are, as what they are. Derrida marks this limit in two ways, beginning in both cases with the withdrawal of the origin. In the first instance he writes: "The absolute invisibility of the origin of the visible, of the good-sun-father-capital, the unattainment of presence or beingness in any form, the whole surplus Plato calls *epekeina tes ousias* (beyond beingness or presence), gives rise to a structure of replacement [*une structure de suppléance*] such that all presences will be supplements substituted for the absent origin . . ." (*D* 193/167). Thus the limit consists in a decisive separation of presences from the origin: set apart from the origin, cut off from it in its invisibility, things present themselves not as themselves but only by way of supplements, only through substitute presences that compensate for the things themselves only at the price of replacing them. Forbidden a view of the origin, one apprehends not the things themselves but only the surrogates that come to take their place. Consequently, Derrida can mark the limit also by referring to these surrogates, or rather, to their way of coming. Here, then, the second indication: the withdrawal "welds dialectic irremediably to its 'inferiors,' the mimetic arts, play, grammar, writing, etc." (*D* 193/167). Forced into complicity with its would-be inferiors, dialectic is unable to keep itself apart from the simulacra put in play by the mimetic arts and by the supplement of writing.

And yet, by Derrida's account, the withdrawal of origin not only limits but also at the same time opens the exercise of dialectic. Onto what is it thereby opened? It is no doubt opened to the play of supplements, to the coming of surrogate presences, that is, to the very domain delimited by the limit. The question is whether dialectic, as it is thus opened, is confined to this domain, or, more precisely, whether, in being exercised within—and in a sense only within—this domain, dialectic is also opened beyond it, even if only to be touched from afar by this *beyond.*

Such opening beyond does not figure prominently in "Plato's Pharmacy." Especially toward the end of the text where the formulations become broader and the reading more synthetic, Derrida seems intent on drawing the limit and on setting dialectic within the confines of this limit. A discourse of non-truth becomes ever more audible, discourse declaring that "the presence of being gets lost, disperses itself, multiplies itself through mimemes, icons, phantasms, simulacra, etc." (*D* 195/168). And yet, there are some indications, brief, almost mute indications, of an opening beyond. One such indication occurs in the context of Derrida's reference to the absolute invisibility of the origin of the visible. Here, as noted already, Derrida declares that this surplus gives rise to supplements replacing the absent origin. But then he adds: "and all differences, within the system of presences, will be the irreducible effect of what remains *epekeina tes ousias*" (*D* 193/167). He does not say how this effect operates, how what is beyond being comes, in its very withdrawal, to effect differentiation in the domain of surrogate presences—only *that* it does so. And though it is this very differentiation that dialectic is bound to trace, nothing is said about how dialectic opens to this effect from beyond.

There is a second indication; it is even slighter, though perhaps more provocative. Recasting the figure of withdrawal, Derrida links it to discourse, declares that it is the precondition of discourse. Referring, then, it seems, to the discourse that ensues in view of the nonvision of origin, he says: "This writing (is) *epekeina tes ousias*" (*D* 194/168). As if to emphasize that this writing itself comes to be determined by its opening to what is beyond being, Derrida sets the *is* in parentheses, just as, in referring to what is beyond being, one would have to modify the copula so as to avoid saying of what is beyond being that it *is.* Yet how writing would be touched by what is ἐπέκεινα τῆς οὐσίας, even to the point of becoming itself ἐπέκεινα τῆς οὐσίας—regarding this there seems to be not the slightest hint.

This figure of the withdrawal as it opens and limits dialectic requires, it seems to me, a response that goes beyond merely doubling it, beyond merely retracing the figure. My proposal is to redraw the figure in a way that amplifies the opening of dialectic to the beyond, its opening toward the origin, toward the ἀρχή. This is not a matter of simply turning against or turning away from what is outlined in Derrida's text; indeed that text needs to be read, even from this point on, with utmost attentiveness and with a sense of its peculiar logic and rigor. Nonetheless, reading the text obliquely, turning its figure this way and that, my aim will be to amplify the opening that, even if only barely, is in play there. In this way I want to begin drawing in another direction that which is here to be thought, that which is being thought in this text, its promise, its *Zusage.* The direction in which I hope to draw it is one that would bring it more thoroughly, more intimately, more rigorously, into connection with the Platonic dialogues.

This venture of amplification can be carried out with precision and coherence only if a certain distinction is marked and the corresponding differentiation is worked out. For in drawing the figure of withdrawal, Derrida mixes two quite distinct Platonic accounts, indeed from two different dialogues that are by no means simply homogeneous either thematically or dramatically. Even if a conflation of these accounts should prove justifiable, at least within certain limits, one would need first of all to distinguish them, to mark their differences. Derrida's reference to the good as ἐπέκεινα τῆς οὐσίας indicates that he is drawing on the account of dialectic found in the central Books of the *Republic.* Yet equally in force in the figure of withdrawal as Derrida outlines it is the passage from the *Phaedo* in which Socrates describes his so-called second sailing (δεύτερος πλοῦς). When, for instance, Derrida declares that vision must be turned away from the origin because of the threat of "mortal blindness by the sun's fires" (*D* 192/166), he is drawing from the account in the *Phaedo*, not that in the *Republic*. Yet, at the same time he is leaving in play the connection that the *Republic* establishes between the good and the sun, a connection that is not made in the *Phaedo* and that cannot be made, granted what Socrates says of the second sailing.

In both dialogues there is a turn back. Yet it is only in the *Phaedo* that the turn back is linked to the threat of blindness. Socrates says that his concern was that he might "suffer the very thing those people do who behold and look at the sun during an eclipse" (*Phaedo* 99d). Thus, like those who, to avoid ruining their eyes, look only at the sun's images in water or something else of the sort, Socrates turns away and looks to λόγοι in order to carry out proper and safe apprehension. Yet what he turns away from and eventually comes back to apprehend in their truth is designated simply as beings (τὰ ὄντα) and described primarily as the kind of things that one usually seeks to apprehend through the senses; these are the things that Socrates had unsuccessfully sought to explain in the investigations of nature (φύσις) with which he began and about which, at this point in the *Phaedo*, he has just told. These things are, most assuredly, not ἐπέκεινα τῆς οὐσίας.

The difference between this passage and the corresponding passage in the *Republic* could not be more striking. There is the difference, first of all, with regard to that from which in each case one turns back: in the *Phaedo* beings; in the *Republic* that which is beyond being. Furthermore, in the *Republic* there is no mention whatsoever of the threat of blindness as compelling one to turn away. Rather, in Socrates' description of the course followed by the prisoner who escapes the cave and eventually, from the earth's surface, casts his vision upward, the culmination is expressed in these words: "Then finally I suppose he would be able to look upon the sun, not its appearance in water or in some alien abode, but the sun itself by itself in its own place and to behold how it is" (*Rep.* 516b). When, subsequently, there is a certain need for the escaped prisoner to turn back and eventually reenter the cave, the turn is dictated by factors quite other than the threat of blindness, factors having to do, for instance, with embodiment and with politics; a certain blindness, presumably temporary, becomes an issue only after the prisoner reenters the cave and, accustomed to the brilliant sunlight above, finds it difficult to see in the subterranean darkness.

To declare noetic vision of the good simply impossible is thus to construe matters otherwise than they are construed in the *Republic*, in the sole Platonic discourse on the good as ἐπέκεινα τῆς οὐσίας. It is equally problematic to refer to the absolute invisibility of the origin of the visible and, on the basis of the alleged remoteness and unattainability of the origin, to conclude that all presences must be merely supplements taking the place of the absent origin. Not that one could justify asserting that the good is simply present to a noetic vision. If the analogy is sustained so that looking upon the good is like looking upon the sun itself, then one may conclude that vision of the good could never be more than momentary. Just as one cannot, except during an eclipse, endure looking at the sun for more than a moment, so, if the analogy is sustained, one could never catch more than a momentary glimpse of the good itself by itself, that is, in its capacity to bestow being and truth upon everything that is. In this case one's vision would achieve, not an intuition filled with some abiding presence, but rather only an instantaneous opening to the good as it bestows its gift of being, its gift to all beings, its gift of being and truth to all beings. To catch sight of the good in this manner is to gain an intimation of it in its generosity.[18]

From beyond being, the good bestows its gifts of being and truth. The two gifts are not separate, not distinct. To bestow ἀλήθεια, unconcealment, upon beings is to let those beings show themselves as being what they are; it is to let them be manifest in their being. To become manifest in their being is precisely not to show themselves only as images utterly apart from their

---

18. To the extent that the good can be submitted to determination—the limits being prescribed precisely by its withdrawal—it is to be determined by reference to this generosity and not in terms of modern concepts of values. See the discussion in chapter 2.

original and their origin; to show themselves as being what they are is precisely not to appear only as simulacra. It is rather to show themselves in such a way that their very whatness, their what-being, their εἶδος, shines through them.

What the good lets come forth—if never simply into presence, if never without the engagement also of λόγος—are the ones in their distinctness over against the swirl of seemingly indeterminate opposites. Yet precisely as they come forth, the one beings come also to shine through the swirl of opposites so as to let even what remains within this swirl nonetheless appear as what it is, that is, show itself in its (limited) determinateness.[19]

It is not inappropriate, then, to say that the good withholds itself from our vision, yielding us only the merest glimpse, yet a glimpse that makes all the difference. The good withdraws from direct vision, from intuition of it as—or as if it were—something stably present; it deflects our vision. Yet because vision opens to it, if only in the moment (ἐξαίφνης), because we catch sight of its gifts of being and unconcealment, our apprehension is drawn beyond the mere play of supplements, of surrogate presences, of images that would be no more than simulacra. As Socrates expresses it in the corresponding discourse in the *Theaetetus* the soul is thereby *stretched*—or is enticed to stretch itself (ἐπορέγεται)—toward being (see *Theaet.* 186a). And from being it returns differently to things, returns to them in their being.

Derrida writes not only of withdrawal (*le retrait*) but also of disappearance (*la disparition*). He writes of them as though they were virtually the same, as though he were only repeating: "To repeat: the disappearance of the good-father-capital-sun is thus the precondition of discourse" (*D* 194/168). Yet disappearance is not quite the same as withdrawal: whatever disappears is simply gone without leaving a trace of itself, whereas what withdraws may, in its very withdrawing, continue to offer some index of itself. That which withdraws may even, as Heidegger says, "draw

19. For further elaboration of this issue, see chapter 2.

us along" in its withdrawing²⁰—especially if it is that which, conferring the gift of being, holds out its promise and evokes our preoriginary *yes*.

Another figure, a reconfiguration, thus begins to take shape, a figure in which the opening to the beyond is amplified—an opening to the beyond of being but also, indeed consequently, an opening beyond the domain—if there be one—in which there would be only a play of supplements, a coming and going of surrogate presences. Now it is the figure of a withdrawal that, from beyond being, draws us to being. It is the figure of a withdrawal in which the good grants a momentary vision of itself in its generosity, opening our vision—and dialectic itself—thereby to things in their being, to showings in which the εἶδος of each thing shines in and through the thing, letting it appear as it determinately is. It is the figure of a withdrawal that draws the soul along, that stretches it toward a beyond to which it can gain a certain proximity but which never comes simply to be present before it.

>>><<<

In view of this figure, one could envisage still another discourse that would complement "Plato's Pharmacy," even if at some point it might prove to be at odds with it. This discourse, too, would be a kind of companion piece, one following still the lines of the *Phaedrus* but now focused on myth—hence a λόγος on μῦθος, literally a mythology. This mythology, extending and confronting "Plato's Pharmacy" by recourse to the dialogue, would compensate somewhat for the fact that Derrida's text passes over almost the entirety of the *Phaedrus* in order to deal primarily with the brief concluding section on writing.

Not that Derrida ignores what is said of myth in the *Phaedrus* prior to the concluding myth of Theuth's invention of writing.

---

20. "Was sich uns entzieht, zieht uns dabei gerade mit, ob wir es sogleich und überhaupt merken oder nicht" (Heidegger, *Was heisst Denken?* [Tübingen: Max Niemeyer, 1954], 5).

On the contrary, the very first section of "Plato's Pharmacy" already broaches this theme. Derrida focuses on the passage, near the beginning of the *Phaedrus* (229a–30a), where Socrates and Phaedrus, walking in the countryside outside Athens, going alongside the Ilissus, consider whether the place they have reached is the spot where Boreas is said to have carried off Orithyia. When Socrates answers that the spot is a bit farther downstream, Phaedrus inquires whether Socrates believes this myth to be true. Socrates responds by speaking of how the σοφοί (wise men—but said, no doubt, ironically), disbelieving such stories, go about explaining that Boreas, the North Wind, blew Orithyia down from the rocks as she was playing with Pharmakeia and that when she had died in this manner she was said to have been carried off by Boreas. Voicing a kind of mock praise for such explanations, Socrates goes on to mention some of the other creatures and indeed monsters that will flood over the σοφοί, requiring explanation, which in turn will require leisure (σχολή). Socrates declares that he, however, has no leisure, because he is not yet able, as the Delphic inscription has it, to know himself. Since—he says—it would be laughable to investigate other things while he is still ignorant of himself, he dismisses these things and accepts whatever is said about them, so as to devote himself instead to knowing himself.

In this brief but pivotal discourse there are several moments that Derrida underlines and that figure significantly in the later developments in "Plato's Pharmacy." Especially notable in this regard is the name Pharmakeia, which first broaches the question of the *pharmakon*; also significant is the reference to the Delphic injunction, that is, to something written that is the source of the Socratic imperative of self-knowledge. Derrida calls attention also to the word χαίρειν, by which Socrates describes the stance that he takes toward the myths or toward the things that are told of in the myths and that are explained in a different way by the σοφοί. The word χαίρειν means primarily: to dismiss, to send off, to say farewell to. Socrates gives the myths a send-off, or, as Derrida writes a bit playfully, he salutes them, sends them on vacation, puts them on leave. Regarding this send-off of the myths, Derrida stresses two points. The first is that the send-off "takes place *in the name of truth*: that is, in the name of knowledge of truth and, more precisely, of truth in the knowledge of the self" (*D* 77/69). The second point is that this dismissal of myth will be interrupted twice so as to welcome back the fable of the cicadas and the myth about the invention of writing.

Both points need to be amplified and indeed turned, developed, in a somewhat different direction. Regarding the first, it is imperative to consider just what it is that Socrates dismisses or sends off. Though the references to these things by way of the pronoun ταῦτα and the phrase περὶ αὐτῶν are indefinite, what is decisive is Socrates' declaration that he accepts, trusts, relies on the customary beliefs about such things (πειθόμενος δὲ τῷ νομιζομένῳ περὶ αὐτῶν) (*Phaedr.* 230a). Clearly the sense is that he accepts, trusts, relies on, the customary beliefs about the various creatures and monsters that the σοφοί seek to explain; indeed the word χαίρειν means not only *to send off* but also *to welcome*, and therefore the send-off could—engaging both senses—be also a welcoming. In any case, what Socrates sends off, dismisses, says farewell to, are not the myths but the attempt to explain, in the manner of the σοφοί, what is told of in the myths. Socrates does not posit an opposition between the myths and the imperative of self-knowledge. Rather, he welcomes the myths in the name of self-knowledge; he puts the myths in service to self-knowledge, as one can see, in the most direct fashion, in the passage about the send-off. Having declared that he investigates, not these things, but himself, he continues: "in order to know whether I am a monster more complicated and furious than Typhon or a gentler and simpler creature" (*Phaedr.* 230a). What, in effect, he proposes is a measuring of self with respect to Typhon, who, according to the myths—which Socrates declares he accepts—was the most frightful offspring of earth and who rose up against Zeus and was killed by Zeus' thunderbolt.

There are also other pertinent references. As, at the very moment when Socrates concludes his remarks about the myths, they reach the spot toward which they have been walking, Socrates swears in the name of Hera: "By Hera, a beautiful resting place" (*Phaedr.* 230b). He identifies it also as a place sacred to some nymphs as well as to Achelous. It is as if gods and other such beings were all around, at least at this place under the plane tree beside the Ilissus. Yet, what is much more significant in breaking down any apparent opposition between the myths and the imperative of self-knowledge is Socrates' relation to the Delphic Oracle. To be sure, the passage in the *Phaedrus* refers explicitly to the Delphic inscription (Τὸ Δελφικὸν γράμμα) (*Phaedr.* 229e), and Derrida justifiably stresses the link that is thus installed between a certain writing and the Socratic imperative of self-knowledge. Yet it is necessary to stress also that through the connection to Delphi there is also established a relation to Apollo, so that it is something told of in the myths—namely, the god—that provides the basis for the imperative of self-knowledge. Indeed it was not just the Delphic inscription "Know yourself" that propelled Socrates on his mission of self-knowledge; but rather, as he explains in the *Apology,* what sent him on his way was the voice of the god as sounded in the Pythia's declaration that there was none wiser than Socrates. It was Apollo—not only through the inscription on his temple but also, more decisively, through his voice—that set Socrates on his way of self-knowledge, a way that was nothing less than service to Apollo.[21]

Such setting of myth in service to self-knowledge is not an isolated occurrence in the *Phaedrus* but permeates, indeed structures, much of the dialogue. Indeed, in reference to Derrida's second point, the myth of the cicadas and that of the invention of writing represent very significant moments in the development of the dialogue. And yet, the great myth of the soul with its image of the charioteer driving his two horses, the myth that constitutes

21. When, speaking before his judges, Socrates begins to tell of the sort of wisdom attributed to him, he is interrupted twice by noisy disturbances from the judges, provoked as they are by what he is saying, especially by his appeal to the authority of Delphi and his proposal to make the god himself witness to Socratic wisdom. See *Apol.* 20d–23c, with my discussion in *Being and Logos,* chap. 1.

the core of Socrates' second speech, his palinode, is incompara-
bly more consequential for the dialogue. Long before Socrates
tells the little stories about how the cicadas sing themselves to
death and about how Thamus rejected the letters invented by
Theuth, he will already have told the elaborate tale about the soul,
responding thereby to the imperative of self-knowledge. In this
tale he will have answered mythically the opening question of the
dialogue: Ὦ φίλε Φαῖδρε, ποῖ δὴ καὶ πόθεν; [Dear Phaedrus,
where are you going and where have you been?—or, translating
with the same economy as the Greek: where to and where from?
whither and whence?]. As in many other dialogues, this very first
line serves to open the broadest horizons of the dialogue as a
whole. Even though it is here addressed singularly to Phaedrus
and even though Phaedrus' immediate answer ("From Lysias,
Socrates, the son of Cephalus; and I am going for a walk outside the wall") offers only the slightest hint at the full amplitude
that the question and the mythical response to it will later attain, nonetheless one can hear in these words the question of the
whither and the whence of the human soul, of the whither and
the whence that mark the limits of self-knowledge.[22]

It is precisely at these limits that the knotting together of knowledge and myth becomes most prominent and most decisive;
yet it is never simply a matter of situating knowledge or λόγος
between these limits and myth beyond them.

The operation of these limits is nowhere more evident than in
Socrates' second speech, his palinode, at the heart of the *Phaedrus*.
Here it must suffice merely to mark, indeed all too lightly, the
connection between this speech and the configuration that took
shape in relation to the withdrawal of the good and the opening
of dialectic.

Attention needs to be given, in particular, to the mythical account of the soul, to the image of the charioteer conveyed by his
two horses through the heaven. It is around this image that the

22. The opening section of the *Phaedrus* is analyzed in much greater detail, as is the
myth in Socrates' second speech, in *Being and Logos*, chap. 3.

entirety of Socrates' speech—and, some would venture to say, the entirety of the *Phaedrus*—is gathered. It is also by way of this image that the *Phaedrus,* in its broadest amplitude, can be brought to communicate with the discourse on the withdrawing of the good and the opening of dialectic, the discourse launched in "Plato's Pharmacy" but also, now, amplified and given an oblique turn.

The beginning of Socrates' second speech reveals immediately that what is to come will concern the sendings of the good. These sendings come only when we are drawn beyond ourselves, only when we are struck with divine madness, with a μανία given us by the gods. In Socrates' words: "Now the greatest of goods [τὰ μέγιστα τῶν ἀγαθῶν] come to us through madness [διὰ μανίας], when it is given by the gods" (*Phaedr.* 244a). A little etymological fancy is made to attest to the nobility of divine madness. Playing on the similarity between μανία (madness) and μαντεία (prophecy), or rather, reconstruing it as the similarity between μανική (manic art) and μαντική (prophetic art), Socrates displays in language a trace that shows that the men of old who invented names regarded μανία, when it comes from the gods, as something noble; for these fancied inventors of names connected—says Socrates—the word μανία with the τέχνη that foretells the future. If today this is not recognized, it is only because nowadays people tastelessly insert the letter ταυ so that the manic art (μανική) of foretelling the future comes to be called the mantic art (μαντική) and hence gets dissociated from μανία. In this little play of etymology, what is most significant is the link established between μανία and the prophetic power of seeing beyond the present, beyond what is present (to sense) in the present. The establishment of this link serves to confirm the character of μανία as being drawn beyond oneself.

The myth itself tells of being drawn beyond oneself, tells of it as an occurrence belonging to a past that would never have been the present of an embodied human being. In that past the soul was like a pair of winged horses and a charioteer. Following in the train of the gods, the souls of humans-to-be soared upward, even if with difficulty; and as they came to the top of the heaven, their vision feasted on the beings themselves in their unconcealment. In Socrates' words, from the heart of the myth: "For the soul that has never seen this unconcealment [ἀλήθεια] can never pass into human form. For a human being must understand what is said according to εἶδος [κατ' εἶδος λεγόμενον], going from a plurality of perceptions to what is gathered into one by reckoning [λογισμῷ]; this is a remembering [ἀνάμνησις] of those things that our soul once saw when traveling in the company of a god." Socrates says that thought (διάνοια), as exemplified in the philosopher, consists in his "always being, insofar as he is able, near to those things by means of memory [μνήμη]" (*Phaedr.* 249b–c). In other words, the philosopher is one who exercises the limited capacity (Socrates says: κατὰ δύναμιν) to be near, in proximity to—which is *not* to say: present to—those things once seen in the absolute past. Socrates concludes this major part of his speech by declaring that what he has said has been said in honor of memory, as a tribute to memory.

In the main passage describing memory, as previously in certain passages from the *Republic,* there is need to insist on the translation of ἀλήθεια as *unconcealment.* Even if the broader question, pursued by Heidegger especially in his debate with Friedländer, as to whether the sense of ἀλήθεια as ὁμοίωσις is also to be found (perhaps even as dominant) in Plato is left open, there can be little doubt but that in the present passage the word has the sense of unconcealment. For the vision of which this passage speaks is of such an anterior character that there would be nothing whatsoever with which what is seen could sustain a relation of likeness or correspondence.

The absolutely anterior vision is required of one who is to be human. It is required in order that, as humans must, one be capable of a certain understanding, of a certain bringing or setting together (ξυνιέναι, the infinitive form of συνίημι, carries both meanings). That which a human must be capable of understanding or bringing together is described as: κατ' εἶδος λεγόμενον. The description has a double meaning. It can mean: understanding that which is said, that which someone says, by referring it to an εἶδος—thus understanding it by recourse to an εἶδος in terms of which it becomes understandable. But the description can also mean: understanding something that, in its way of being said, is said according to, by reference to, an εἶδος. Since indeed whatever is said is said according to an εἶδος and since, accordingly, one could understand it only by reference to the εἶδος, both senses of the description must be in play. In the passage a parallel description is given starting, not from something said, but from perception (αἴσθησις). Here again a transition is marked, an understanding that brings or sets together a manifold of perceptions by proceeding to a one gathered by λογισμός. The word can mean reckoning, as in arithmetic, or even counting, as indeed would be expected, considering that it is a matter of ones. But the word can also be used without reference to number, counting, or calculation, and then it is the connection with λόγος that becomes decisive. Yet this connection is no less to be expected, since that which, first of all and decisively, gathers into ones is precisely λόγος, as when, in saying *tree,* one gathers into the one thing meant everything that can be called by this name.

This understanding, this bringing or setting together, is said to be a remembering. Memory is no pure vision, but rather, as the above analysis has shown, it proceeds from, through, and to speech, that is, it is permeated by λόγος. To this extent one cannot but agree with what Derrida says of memory, that it is "by its essence finite," that "memory always already needs signs in order to recall the non-present, to which it necessarily has a relation." Derrida expresses memory's need of signs by referring to memory as contaminated: it is as if one would have expected memory to be pure vision, pure self-presence, but then finds that this purity has been compromised by the intrusion of signs. But who would have dreamed that memory is pure self-presence devoid of signs? Derrida suggests that it was precisely Plato who sustained this dream: "But what Plato *dreams* of is a memory with no sign [*une mémoire sans signe*]" (*D* 124/109). That such can hardly be the case is attested by the above passage on memory, a passage taken from the heart of the mythical account of the soul.

In any case, the myth tells of the opening beyond; it tells of how the soul is stretched toward being, set into proximity to being. Through this opening it becomes possible for the manifold of sense to be gathered into a one being, so that things can show themselves, not merely as simulacra, but as being, in their being. What the *Republic* delimits as momentary vision of the withdrawing origin is told of in the great myth of the *Phaedrus* as memory reenacting a flight and a vision projected into an absolute past, as a remembering in which we are drawn beyond ourselves, as manic memory, as memory enabled by the madness sent as gift from the gods.

>>><<<

At the third of the three sites outlined at the beginning, the force of Derrida's thought is deployed around the single word—if it be a word—χώρα. This single would-be word also entitles the text linked primarily to this site. Various passageways leading to this site have already been discerned, most notably in connection with the *pharmakon*: above all, the way in which, at certain points at least, the discourse on the *pharmakon* tends to mutate into the question of a third kind; also, more specifically, the question whether in the passage from the pharmacological swirl of opposites to the fundamental distinction of Platonism there is a remainder, something that could never be enclosed, comprehended, by the opposition between intelligible and sensible, something neither intelligible nor sensible; or, to put it otherwise, the question whether the bottomless fund (*fonds sans fond*) of the *pharmakon* remains itself withdrawn from the sphere that is taken to define Platonism.

It is difficult to know where to begin with the χώρα. This is especially the case if one observes that in the *Timaeus* itself Timaeus stipulates: "With regard to everything it is most important to begin at the natural beginning" (*Tim.* 29b). Most remarkably, the *Timaeus* itself does not begin at the natural beginning; rather, even Timaeus himself is compelled twice to interrupt his discourse and make another beginning. In a sense beginning at the natural beginning would seem to mean beginning precisely with the χώρα; for the χώρα is before all things, before the birth of the heaven (πρὸ τῆς οὐρανοῦ γενέσεως) (*Tim.* 48b), hence already in a kind of time before time itself; it is a kind of nature before nature, so that it is preeminently the natural beginning. Yet the *Timaeus* does not begin with the χώρα; rather, the discourse on the χώρα is first broached in the wake of an interruption, in a palentropic recoil into another beginning, a beginning that is made by turning back to a still earlier beginning, one still more anterior.

Still more perplexing difficulties are posed by the recoil of the χώρα upon the speech that would be about it, that is, by the way in which its character—or rather, lack of character—places on speech demands that exceed its usual capacities. The question cannot be evaded: What kind of speech would be suited to saying the χώρα? Derrida begins his text *Khôra* with an apparent expectation that the answer to this question can be determined by way of the opposition between λόγος and μῦθος, specifically that the saying of the χώρα takes the form of μῦθος. But, in the course of his inquiry, it becomes ever more evident that the discourse on the χώρα, while having in a way the look of myth ("this discourse reminds us of a sort of myth within the myth, of an open abyss in the general myth"), is in the end "heterogeneous with myth."[23] It is neither λόγος nor μῦθος (see *K* 76/117). It seems indeed that this opposition is quite insufficient for characterizing Timaeus' discourses. Even in the preliminary speeches

23. Derrida, *Khôra* (Paris: Galilée, 1993), 68. Translated by Ian McLeod in *On the Name*, ed. Thomas Dutoit (Stanford: Stanford University Press, 1995), 113. The first version of the French text appeared in *Poikilia: Études offertes à Jean-Pierre Vernant* (Paris: EHESS, 1987). The book version (1993) does not differ substantially from the earlier text; in the book Derrida merely adds an initial paragraph, divides the text in a slightly different way, and introduces a few minor reformulations. The prominence of the theme of myth in Derrida's text is likely related to its having been a contribution to a collection honoring Jean-Pierre Vernant; the epigraph consists of a lengthy citation from Vernant's "Raisons du mythe." Further references to *Khôra* will be indicated by the abbreviation *K*, followed by the page numbers in the French and English editions, respectively.

by Socrates and Critias, where this opposition is still posed—as
the opposition between a true λόγος and an invented μῦθος—a
kind of reversal and perhaps redetermination of the opposition
is under way. For Socrates' account of the paradigmatic city is
called an invented μῦθος, whereas the old, handed-down story
that Critias tells about some largely forgotten ancestors is called
a true λόγος (*Tim.* 26e).[24] In and with reference to Timaeus'
discourse, the words λόγος and μῦθος continue to be used but
with a curious vacillation that does not at all accord with the
traditional distinction.[25] One can hardly avoid concluding that
what is at issue in the *Timaeus* cannot be caught in this net.

Indeed the *Timaeus* itself proposes another schema, a threefold schema corresponding to the three kinds distinguished in
Timaeus' second discourse. There is, first, the discourse that says
the paradigmatic εἴδη, the selfsame beings, and that is itself stable, sharing in the character of that of which it speaks. Secondly,
there is the kind of discourse that concerns sensible images.
Timaeus calls it εἰκὼς λόγος. Since it is speech about images
(εἰκών), it can be called *image discourse, discourse on likenesses.* Or
the designation can be translated *likely discourse,* though only if
this expression is totally dissociated from the probable; for the
character of such discourse is determined by its orientation to
images and has nothing to do with probability. What Timaeus
says of the χώρα often takes the form of εἰκὼς λόγος, even of
an εἰκὼς λόγος that is—directly or indirectly—designated as
such. For example, immediately following the declaration that
they must speak more clearly (σαφέστερον) about these things,
Timaeus launches a discourse in which the χώρα is portrayed in
the image of gold, in the likeness of a mass of gold that is modeled into all possible figures or shapes (see *Tim.* 50a–b). Yet as the
discourse proceeds toward what can be rigorously designated as
the chorology (*Tim.* 52a–d), a third kind of discourse comes into
play. It is a discourse whose legitimacy cannot be established,

24. See my discussion in *Chorology,* 39.
25. Ibid., 97 n. 6.

and indeed Timaeus refers to it as bastard (*Tim.* 52b). In Athenian usage a bastard (νόθος) was the child of a citizen father and an alien mother. Perhaps, then, the chorology is the offspring of citizen Timaeus as he addresses the alien of aliens. And yet, Timaeus is from Locri; he is indeed a citizen but not of Athens. Perhaps, then, the bastard speech is the offspring of another father, another who is called father, namely, the first kind, the intelligible εἴδη. Perhaps, then, this speech arises only through one who invokes this father to consort with the wandering, erring alien mother.

Even now, even still, we have not made a proper beginning. Still, we have not managed to begin at the beginning. Still, we have not—in the present discussion—arrived at the point from which one could begin with the χώρα. Rather, we have, at best, gone wandering between the χώρα and the speech that would say it—gone wandering in a way that resembles more the movement of the mother than the upright bearing of the father. Let us wander on a bit more and turn to Derrida's text *Khôra*, not beginning at the beginning but well along in the text. Derrida writes of how so many interpretations have come to give form to the χώρα, to say what it is, to leave their mark on it. Yet all miss the mark, because on the χώρα there is no mark, that is, it receives every mark yet takes none to itself, remains itself unmarked. The χώρα is both utterly promiscuous and yet, as Derrida stresses, virginal. Regarding the names *receptacle* and χώρα, which Timaeus brings to bear on it, Derrida comments: "these names do not designate an essence, the stable being of an *eidos*, since *khôra* is neither of the order of the *eidos* nor of the order of mimemes, that is, of images of the *eidos* which come to imprint themselves in it—which thus *is not*, not belonging to the two known or recognized genera of being" (*K* 28/95). In short, the χώρα is neither an intelligible being (an εἶδος) nor a sensible being, but rather a third kind. One will hesitate to say even that it is a third kind *of being*; this is why Derrida stresses that "it is not"—and so, as he continues, "*Khôra* is not, above all not [*n'est pas, surtout pas*], a support or a subject that *would give* place by receiving or by conceiving" (*K* 28f. /95—translation significantly altered). The χώρα is not a being—neither substance nor subject—in which other beings have a place and so come to pass, even though Timaeus indeed declares that it is that in which (ἐν ᾧ) generated things come to be and from which (ἐκεῖθεν) they perish. Yet it is an *in which* and a *from which* that *is not,* that is not a being, not even—strictly speaking—a being of a third kind. Even to call it a kind, even if not of being, is to submit it to the first kind in a way that is not warranted, since kind as such (γένος) is determined by the first kind; that is, it is precisely the character of beings of the first kind that each is a kind and delimits a kind.

Still further, the χώρα is that which, though it *is not* (is not a being), can, according to Timaeus, be said to be—in a litany that holds virtually everything in reserve—invisible, formless, everlasting, all-receiving, such as to partake of the intelligible in the most perplexing way, and—sealing the litany—most difficult to catch. It can be said in these ways provided all manner of artifices of avoidance are put in play—even if only in imagination, even if without being inscribed—so as to cross out every *is* and every other designation that would assimilate the χώρα to the two kinds of beings. Writing with such artifices would not be perverse but rather would constitute the only way of composing such bastard discourse as is demanded by the χώρα.

In such a discourse it might, then, be said: while the χώρα is not even a being, much less an enclosure in which and from which things would come to pass, it is that in which all generated beings, all things of sense, must come to be if they are to be at all, thereby, as the chorology itself says, "clinging to being at least in a certain way, on pain of being nothing at all" (*Tim.* 52c). Only in this way can these phantoms, which are utterly apart from all selfsame being, nonetheless somehow *be.* It is in this connection that one could propose—though nothing like this expression occurs in the *Timaeus*—to call the χώρα the outside or exteriority of being. Whereas the first kind is interiority as such, not in the sense of subjectivity but in the sense that being, in its selfsameness, turns immediately back into itself, exteriority can erupt only in and through the χώρα.[26] For by coming to be in the χώρα, the phantoms that are apart from, utterly exterior to, selfsame being can nonetheless in their very exteriority *be*.

One could say, further, that through the introduction of the χώρα into the basic Platonic schema, there is achieved, at the most anterior stage, a stabilizing of the opposition between interior and exterior, between inside and outside. The question, then, would be whether the stabilizing of this opposition at this stage would not serve to stabilize, to some degree, all other oppositions, halting or at least limiting the incursions that belong to the operation of the *pharmakon*.[27]

One could say, finally, circling back to the configuration that took shape obliquely from "Plato's Pharmacy," that it is by virtue of the χώρα that things can show themselves, not merely as simulacra, but rather as what they are, in their being. By coming to pass in the χώρα, things, though apart from being, can come forth as images of the being that is apart, can show themselves as being what they are. Or rather, they can thus show themselves,

26. It is curious that in "Plato's Pharmacy" Derrida broaches this issue but without referring it to discourse on the χώρα. He writes: "What is is not what it is, identical and identical to itself, unique, unless it *adds to itself* the possibility of being *repeated* as such. And its identity is hollowed out by that addition, withdraws itself in the supplement that presents it" (*D* 194/168). Yet the χώρα is precisely what allows there to be such repetition, allows it to take place as a repetition that is apart from being and that consequently does not compromise, does not "hollow out," being as such. The emphasis that Derrida places on repetition as defining the eidetic—hence as belonging to it rather than occurring apart—goes back to the late works of Husserl and to Derrida's studies of these works, especially of "The Origin of Geometry." This emphasis is succinctly expressed in "Plato's Pharmacy": "The *eidos* is that which can always be repeated as *the same*. The ideality and invisibility of the *eidos* are its power-to-be-repeated" (*D* 141/123). If, on the other hand, the eidetic is determined primarily by selfsameness—as it is in the *Timaeus*—its undoing through the necessity of repetition is averted.

27. Derrida writes: "Plato thinks of writing and tries to comprehend it, to dominate it, on the basis of *opposition* as such. In order for these contrary values (good/evil, true/false, essence/appearance, inside/outside, etc.) to be in opposition, each of the terms must be simply *external* to the other, which means that one of these oppositions (inside/outside) must already be accredited as the matrix of all possible opposition" (*D* 117/103). The question is how far the stabilizing achieved by introducing the χώρα would go toward accrediting the opposition inside/outside as such a matrix.

provided we who apprehend them have caught a glimpse of being
as such or have reenacted the visionary flight up to being that the
great myth projects into an absolute past, remembering in our
god-sent madness what lies apart in its selfsameness.

>>><<<

My discussions with Jacques Derrida about the χώρα go back
to 1982–83. At that time he gave me a copy of the typescript
of his text *Khôra*, which appeared in print only in 1987. This
generous gift was not entirely unsolicited, as our mutual interest
in the *Timaeus* had, more than once, come up in conversations
that year in Paris. Many years later, referring to our dialogue, he
wrote that the *Timaeus* is "a text which we both feel possesses an
implosive power which it keeps in reserve."[28] It is not of course
a matter only of the single word. Derrida insists on contextual-
ization; he stresses that the development of a concept, indeed its
very delimitation, requires, not mere designation, but inscription
within an extended discourse, within a text.[29] Nonetheless, there
can be little question but that, within the text of the *Timaeus*,
preeminently within the second of Timaeus' three discourses,
the word χώρα bears the weight of what is there thought, of
what is thought in a thinking so exorbitant that what is there
thought can no longer even be called—except very improperly—
a concept. This word, if it be a word in this context, is the fuse
that would have set off—and that now again could be made to
set off—the implosion of the dyadic structure of intelligible and
sensible that otherwise Platonism would be taken to have be-
queathed to the entire history of metaphysics. This no doubt is
the implosive power Derrida had in mind.

The next phase of the dialogue—at least the next public
phase—took place at Cerisy in 1992, at the extended colloquium
"*autour du travail de Jacques Derrida*" organized by Marie-Louise

---

28. Derrida, "Comme si c'était possible," 522; English version in *Questioning Derrida*, 111.

29. See Derrida, "Comme si c'était possible," 510; English version in *Questioning
Derrida*, 102.

Mallet under the title "Le passage des frontières." In my brief presentation[30] and in the discussion, primarily with Jacques Derrida, that followed, two issues arose. The first had to do with the definite article, with whether χώρα should be written with or without the definite article. In his text, the title of which omits the article, Derrida maintains that the article should be omitted, that one should write (in the transliteration used in the book version of his text) *khôra*, not *the khôra*. He had explained that the definite article presupposes the existence of a thing, to which one would refer by adding the article to the general name. The name *khôra*, on the other hand, does not—as *Khôra* explains—designate any of the recognized types of existents; what it would designate is neither intelligible nor sensible, and according to the philosophical discourse that has always governed logic and grammar, there are no existents other than those that fall under one or the other of these types. Much later, in his last words on this question, Derrida is still more direct: "There is, here, in the singular case of *khora* . . . a name without a referent, without a referent that is a thing or a being [*étant*] or even a phenomenon appearing *as such*."[31]

My initial concern—hence my decision to entitle my contribution "De la Chora"—was that to omit the article would risk effacing all difference between the word and that of which the word would speak, collapsing it thus into itself. If the word can be linked neither to a referent in the usual sense (a sensible being) nor to a meaning or a signified (an intelligible being), then must it not—in order to remain in any sense a word, in order not to revert to mere sound incapable of saying anything—be linked to something else, something that it says, even if not to a being that is either sensible or intelligible, even if not to a being at all? In order for there to be a discourse on (the) χώρα, the word must say, beyond itself, something that, while beyond being—or perhaps,

30. "De la Chora," in *Le passage des frontières* (Paris: Galilée, 1994), 173–77. English version: "Of the χώρα," *Epoché* 2 (1994): 1–12.

31. Derrida, "Comme si c'était possible," 523; English version: *Questioning Derrida*, 111.

before being (the dialogue on this point was to be resumed)—
nonetheless appears, however minimally, however obliquely.

In the lecture "De la Chora," presented at Cerisy, I ventured
some indications regarding such appearing, suggesting above all,
that it must be an appearing in which what appears (the χώρα)
does not appear *as such*, even though it precisely (the χώρα)
is what appears. Thus I granted Derrida's point, clarified for
me through the discussion, that (the) χώρα was—in his later
formulation—not "even a phenomenon appearing *as such*." But,
as I elaborated only later in the much more developed context
of *Chorology*, there is nonetheless an appearing of this so-called
third kind when, for instance, inflamed in part, it appears as
fire.[32]

In our dialogue at Cerisy there was a second issue. It concerned a statement in *Khôra* that occurs in the same context as
the remarks about the definite article. Derrida writes: *"Il y a khôra,
mais la khôra n'existe pas"* (*K* 32/97). In this same context Derrida
mentions, with some caution, the *es gibt*; though he refers here
to negative theology, it seemed to me that there was clearly an
allusion to Heidegger. This was, then, the question I posed: that
of the connection between the *il y a* (in the expression *"il y a
khôra"*) and the *es gibt* (as in the Heideggerian expressions *"es
gibt Sein," "es gibt Zeit"*). Derrida vigorously denied that the *il y
a* could be rendered by *es gibt*, insisting rather on differentiating
rigorously between what comes from a giving (even in the withdrawal of that which gives, the withdrawal that belongs to the
very condition of giving as such) and what, like (the) χώρα—if
it can be said that anything is like (the) χώρα—is there, is the
very *there* as such, or rather, more precisely, *would* be the *there* as
such, were it possible for the *there* to be as such.

The dialogue continued in Derrida's essay "Tense." The differentiation that—for me at least—had been sharpened by our
discussion in Cerisy is extended or shifted into a new formulation. To be sure, the differentiation between the *il y a* and the

32. See my *Chorology*, 109.

es gibt remains pertinent, signaling the difference between what comes as gift and (the) χώρα that is (the) there. But now, one term of the difference is attached to the context of the *Republic*: inasmuch as the good, from beyond being, bestows upon all things their being and their truth, it belongs to the order of the gift, set over against that of the *il y a*. One order is that of the free gift of being, the other that of utter reception without gain. Thus, Derrida comes to focus on the relation between what is said in the Platonic discourse on the good—namely, that the good is beyond being (ἐπέκεινα τῆς οὐσίας)—and what goes unsaid in the discourse on (the) χώρα. His question, as he poses it in "Tense," reads: "And yet why does not Plato say that χώρα is ἐπέκεινα τῆς οὐσίας? Why is that so difficult to think?"[33]

My response was to underline the difficulty by referring to the wildness of the χώρα: like an animal in the wild, it is utterly elusive, resisting by its own secret means our every effort to make it appear as such, to force it to be present, and escaping our every means of trying to capture it, to snare it with our concepts. Yet, for all the difficulty in even beginning to bring the designation ἐπέκεινα τῆς οὐσίας to bear on (the) χώρα, there is a sentence in the *Republic* that seems nonetheless to make it imperative to ask about such a bearing. The sentence, which I cited in responding[34] to the question posed by Derrida in "Tense," is the one that played a crucial role above in the discussion of "Plato's Pharmacy," the passage in the discourse on the cave that describes what occurs at the final stage of the prisoner's ascent. Socrates is speaking: "Then finally I suppose he would be able to look upon the sun itself by itself in its χώρα and to behold how it is" (*Rep.* 516b).

In "Daydream" I returned to this passage in order to interrogate the transition it prompts, the transition from what is said about the sun, about seeing it in its χώρα, to what presumably

---

33. Derrida, "Tense." Translated by D. F. Krell in *The Path of Archaic Thinking: Unfolding the Work of John Sallis*, ed. Kenneth Maly (Albany: State University of New York Press, 1995), 73.

34. See my response, "'. . . A Wonder that One Could Never Aspire to Surpass,'" *The Path of Archaic Thinking*, 262.

could be said about the good, that at the pinnacle of the ascent the escaped prisoner sees the good in its χώρα. The most difficult question is perhaps that of the different values that the word must have when linked to the sun and to the good, respectively. The concept of metaphor seems pertinent here, though its pertinence may be displaced somewhat as a result of the level at which the discourse moves: Is the opening of the distinction between intelligible and sensible—as well as the mediation of this difference—not presupposed by the very concept of metaphor? Must there not be at least a certain opening beyond the sensible, a clearing of a certain free space in which the movement can take place between something meant and the metaphor in which it is expressed? Does metaphorizing not itself require a certain space? Is this space thinkable apart from the χώρα? In any case, in moving from the seemingly metaphorical level of the sun to the intelligible level of the good, hence from one value of χώρα to the other, it is not entirely clear whether one merely traces in reverse a metaphorizing or whether one charts the very opening of the possibility of metaphor.

The questions can be posed still more directly. According to the Platonic text, the ascent culminates in a glimpse of the sun in its χώρα. The question—leaving open all the questions just posed about metaphor itself at this level—is, first of all: Does the word χώρα function here as a metaphor, just as the sun functions as a metaphor for the good? In other words, is there a χώρα of the good that is metaphorized in the Platonic text as the χώρα of the sun? And then, secondly, if there is a χώρα of the good,[35] is this to be identified with the χώρα as put forth in the discourse of the *Timaeus*? Conjoined, the two questions ask, in effect: Is the χώρα (of the *Timaeus*) metaphorized as the χώρα of the sun? Can there be a metaphorizing of the χώρα?

To the question, formulated in this way, Derrida answers directly and unambiguously: "The *khora* of the sun, in the *Republic*,

---

35. Here the *there is* would have to be taken as *il y a*, so as to suspend the *is*. It will become evident momentarily that the use of the indefinite article with the word χώρα is highly aporetic.

is not, it seems to me, able to be a metaphorical value for *khora* in the *Timaeus*. Nor, for that matter, the inverse. Although the word clearly designates, in both cases, an 'emplacement' or a 'locality,' there is no analogy, no commensurability possible, it seems to me, between these two places. The word 'place' ['*lieu*'] itself has such a different semantic value in the two cases that their relation... seems to be one of homonymy rather than figurality or synonymy."[36]

Certainly it is the case that the word χώρα has a range of different semantic values in the various Platonic texts. The word occurs with great frequency in the *Laws*. There it has, for the most part, such prephilosophical senses as terrain, landscape, country in the sense of farmland to be cultivated, countryside in distinction from the city proper (πόλις), and country as inclusive both of countryside and city. In the *Republic* less concrete senses are to be found: for instance, when the most talented youth are corrupted and abandon philosophy, then—so it is said—philosophy's χώρα becomes empty. In the *Sophist* the philosopher, intent upon being, is said to have difficulty seeing because of the bright light of this χώρα; so, if, in this passage, χώρα can still be rendered as something like *place*, then the place designated is that of the brightness of being.[37] In this case the sense of the word approaches that found in the passage in question in the *Republic*: through the brightness of its shining, the sun bestows being and truth upon things and therefore is analogous to the good.

There is thus a broad spectrum of senses, ranging from such concrete, prephilosophical designations as that of land or terrain to such eminently nonconcrete, purely ontological significations as that of the place of the brightness of being. In the latter case the topical character of what is designated undergoes a shift: the place of the brightness of being is not a locality where crops could be cultivated (except in a highly metaphorical sense). The shift proceeds still further when, in the *Timaeus*, χώρα is used to designate

36. Derrida, "Comme si c'était possible," 522–23; English version in *Questioning Derrida*, 111.

37. These and other passages in which χώρα occurs are discussed in *Chorology*, 116–17.

the third kind: now the shift is so radical that it produces an eclipse of signification itself, since that which the word χώρα thus comes to mean can be no meaning as such, neither that of a concrete place such as a terrain nor the sense of place conceived as something intelligible. Nonetheless, even in the *Timaeus* the χώρα not only is portrayed through various images in which reception figures most prominently but also, as noted above, is designated as the *in which* (ἐν ᾧ) of sensible things, as that in which, even though they are mere phantoms, they can, still, cling to being rather than being nothing at all. To this extent there remains a certain continuity across the entire spectrum of senses found in the dialogues. There remains a certain unity of sense, even if the eclipse of signification at one extreme renders it a strange unity, indeterminable by the usual procedures of conceptual determination. This continuity, this unity—strange though it be—gets passed over if the relation between different values of the word is reduced to mere homonymy, if one says, for instance, of χώρα as used in the *Republic,* in comparison to the word as used in the *Timaeus,* that "it is only a homonym, almost another word."[38]

On the other hand, it is of utmost importance, it seems to me, to prevent χώρα from settling into a determinate, stable meaning. One will need especially to resist the tendency—driven by the very unity of sense that I have just traced—to let the word take on the sense of place (*lieu*), as historically it did, from Chalcidius on. Sometimes, as in his response to "Daydream," it seems that Derrida gives in to this tendency, which is all the more surprising considering how thoroughly his reading works against any such translation. The problem is that once χώρα slips into being translated as *place,* one will readily say that the *Republic* and the *Timaeus* deal with two different places, almost as if dealing, for instance, with the heaven and the earth. The two places can seem so different—the broad open heaven/the self-

38. Derrida, "Comme si c'était possible," 510; English version in *Questioning Derrida,* 103.

secluding earth, the place from which the greatest of gifts ar-
rive/the place of reception, nurturing, birth—that they will then
seem to lack all commensurability. One could not even serve to
metaphorize the other.

But suppose the χώρα of the *Timaeus* were not taken simply as
the place where all sensible things are and must be in order to be
at all. There is indeed good reason to insist on the difference: at
the very heart of the choric discourse in the *Timaeus*, a difference
is marked between place (τόπος) and the χώρα, and it is declared
that, caught up in a dream, we are unable to distinguish these,
so that the thought of the χώρα gets conflated with the thought
that everything must be in some place (τόπος), that is, with the
thought "that that which is neither on earth nor anywhere in
the heaven is nothing" (*Tim.* 52b).[39] Suppose, then, that one
were to distinguish the χώρα from place by thinking of it as an
instituting operation, as the operation by which something like a
place would first open up; in this guise it would be a happening,
an occurrence, not something done, for instance, by a subject.
Granted the range of senses traced above, such spacing could
be conceived (writing this word with artifice, consigning it to
what the *Timaeus* calls bastard reckoning) at various levels: as
a spacing that clears the space for concrete, sensible things, but
also as a spacing that puts in place the brightness of being. These
spacings would, in turn, be joined by the same strange unity that
gives continuity to the various senses that χώρα was found to
have in the dialogues. A certain affinity with the Heideggerian *es
gibt,* with what Heidegger thinks as *Lichtung,* would, then, not
be excluded.

In the discourse that the *Timaeus* addresses to the χώρα, there
are other moments that work against the tendency to conflate the
χώρα with *place.* Perhaps the most notable moment of this sort is
the image of gold as modeled and remodeled into every possible
figure or shape. Even though, in the most rigorous sense, there
can be no image of the χώρα, the gold as perpetually remodeled

39. See *Chorology,* especially 118–24.

is most certainly presented as a way of saying (and of showing through the saying) what the third kind is, hence providing an image no less improper to it than such words as *what, kind,* and *is.* Along with the image of gold, there is also the image of the χώρα as a matrix (ἐκμαγεῖον) for all things, as like a mass of wax on which a seal can be set—thus, as Derrida no doubt observed, a kind of writing pad, even a mystic writing pad *avant la lettre.* Whereas, historically, both these images contributed to the misconception of the χώρα as ὕλη—indeed its replacement by ὕλη, already effected by Aristotle[40]—if, instead of the underlying material, one stresses the perpetual remodeling and restamping, then these images are suggestive of a way of envisioning the χώρα that takes it rather as an operation, a happening.

Is it the χώρα, operative in such a manner, that grants to the good its abode ἐπέκεινα τῆς οὐσίας?

It is from such thoughts that I would like to have renewed and carried on the dialogue with Jacques Derrida. If, as he said, "we are today on the verge of Platonism" (*D* 122f. /107), could such thought bring us to this Platonism, even if perhaps an unheard-of Platonism, an exorbitant Platonism?

It is perhaps such a Platonism as one might find encrypted in the very final words of the *Phaedo.* Having sung for Echecrates the swan song that Socrates sang on his last day, having reported Socrates' cryptic last words and told finally of his death, Phaedo concludes by calling Socrates "the best and, yes, the most thoughtful and the most just" (*Phaedo* 118). Socrates—ever attendant to his ignorance—had been the most thoughtful regarding what remained in reserve; he had been most thoughtful precisely by being most reserved in thought. And if justice requires rendering to each what is rightfully his, then the superlative can appropriately denote rendering more than the other can rightfully claim, that is, free giving; Socrates had been the most just by being the most generous.

---

40. See ibid., 151–54.

It is on the verge of such Platonism, such perhaps exorbitant Platonism, that I would like to have renewed and continued the dialogue with my friend Jacques Derrida. I know that as I turned, once again, back to these ancient texts, calling again on what they hold still in reserve, he would have smiled. With reserve yet with generosity. The smile of a friend. And, continuing, the voice of the friend.

4

The Politics of Music

Music can mark a significant political event, its performance becoming part of the event itself and attesting musically to the significance of the event. Tan Dun's *Symphony 1997: Heaven, Earth, Mankind* is exemplary in this regard. Commissioned for the celebration of the reunification of Hong Kong with China on July 1, 1997, the symphony attests to—and thus projects hope for—a union without reduction, juxtaposing the tolling of an ancient Chinese bianzhong with, among other sounds, that of a modern Western symphony orchestra.

Music can also memorialize an event or series of events in the life of a significant political figure. It can do so even in such a way as to bring that memory to bear inspiringly on the political situation in which the music is composed and first performed. Thus, amidst the intense patriotism evoked by the Second World War, Aaron Copland composed his *Lincoln Portrait* for speaker and orchestra. While memorializing Lincoln by way of a musical portrayal and certain of his own words, most movingly from the Gettysburg Address, it is designed to project into the wartime in which it was composed a generalized portrait of one who led the country in another time of war.

The case of Dmitri Shostakovich is more complicated and more ambiguous, composing, as he did, during the period of

Stalin's regime. After his very successful opera *Lady Macbeth of Mtsensk* received severe political criticism in two articles in *Pravda* in 1936 (the criticism, which Shostakovich later blamed Stalin for having instigated, charged him with sacrificing to bourgeois formalism the capacity of good music to inspire the masses), he held back his *Fourth Symphony* (not performed until 1962) and turned to the composition of his *Fifth Symphony*. As indicated by the phrase usually associated with it, "a Soviet artist's reply to just criticism," the *Fifth Symphony* is a musical-political response, even though today we know that Shostakovich's relation to the Soviet regime was much more problematic than it once seemed. Much less ambiguous in this respect is the *Seventh Symphony*, composed in 1941 during the siege of Leningrad and reportedly described by Shostakovich himself as "devoted to the ordinary Soviet people, who have become the heroes of the patriotic war."[1]

In every case, whatever the specific intent, music can be politically effective only because it touches humans in an incomparable way. It will be said not only that music touches us but also that it speaks to us in a unique way and that it evokes our feeling as well. And yet, rigorously considered, music is not a matter of touch, of speech, or of feeling; in each of these cases the effect of music—and that is to say, of a certain kind of sound—has been displaced into an entirely different register, metaphorized in the effort to express something that is not entirely homogeneous with language and that will perhaps always to some extent escape verbal expression. Music itself is proverbially resistant to being expressed in words. How much more resistant to such expression is its effect on us!—mere sounds that penetrate to what once

---

1. Sigmund Spaeth, *A Guide to Great Orchestral Music* (New York: Random House, 1943), 387. Spaeth cites also the following from an interview with Shostakovich: "After this preliminary theme... I introduce the main theme, which was inspired by the transformation of these ordinary people into heroes by the outbreak of the war. This builds up into a requiem for those of them who are perishing in the performance of their duty. In the first movement's final passages, I introduce something very intimate, like a mother's tears over her lost children. It is tragic, but it finally becomes transparently clear" (387).

would have been called the depths of the human soul, to what to-day we would perhaps call—drawing metaphorically on music—our most fundamental attunement. The effect of music, which grounds the very possibility of a politics of music, resists the profoundest efforts to think it and to express it.

Yet in some measure it has been thought and has been expressed. And in what is among its most refined expressions, there is echoed—in an echo that, across the centuries, perfects in certain ways the original—the trope in which it was first thought, a trope broached on the verge of philosophy itself.

Its expressive echo perfects the trope by recasting it poetica-lly. In the final Act of *The Merchant of Venice,* Lorenzo says to Jessica:

> How sweet the moonlight sleeps upon this bank!
> Here will we sit and let the sounds of music
> Creep in our ears; soft stillness and the night
> Become the touches of sweet harmony.
>
> (V.i.54–58)

After Lorenzo has ventured a brief discourse on the inaudible music of the heavens, musicians enter. Entreated by Lorenzo, they begin to play and, it seems, continue playing as Lorenzo delivers his discourse on music, speaking of music as music also is played, almost as if his words about music were set to music. He begins with the observation that even a herd of wild colts can be readily tamed by the trumpet's sound. Then he continues:

> Therefore the poet
> Did feign that Orpheus drew trees, stones, and floods;
> Since naught so stockish, hard, and full of rage
> But music for the time doth change his nature.
> The man that hath no music in himself,
> Nor is not moved with concord of sweet sounds,
> Is fit for treasons, stratagems, and spoils;
> The motions of his spirit are dull as night,
> And his affections dark as Erebus.

Let no such man be trusted. Mark the music.
(V.i.79–88)

>>><<<

Socrates' most forceful declaration about the connection between music and politics is strategically placed on the itinerary of the *Republic*. It occurs just before the decisive move with which Socrates brings the founding of cities in λόγος to its completion. This final, decisive move is an avowal of ignorance: we have no knowledge (nor can we be properly informed by others) of what pertains to the burial of the dead, the founding of temples, sacrifices, and the care of gods, daimons, and heroes; and thus, says Socrates, it is necessary to place all such matters in the charge of Apollo, interpreted through his oracle. Once these remaining matters have been assigned to Apollo, as also, in the *Apology*, Socrates' own practice was referred back to Apollo, then Socrates can affirm that the city is completed: "So then, son of Ariston, your city would now be founded" (*Rep.* 427c).

Socrates' declaration about music and politics is bounded on the other side by his outrageous assertion that for the guardians of the city the possession of women, marriage, and procreation of children must be arranged according to the maxim that friends have all things in common. It is precisely this assertion that will later provoke the interruption of the political discourse: at the outset of Book 5, Polemarchus, Adeimantus, and Glaucon insist that they have been waiting for Socrates to explain what he has said about the community of women and children; and, reenacting the mock struggle at the beginning of the dialogue, they vow not to release Socrates until he has given such an explanation. It is this interruption that, in turn, leads, via the comedy of the city, to the long discourse on philosophy that, though treated ironically as a detour, constitutes the core of the dialogue. Yet what is equally curious is that on the very heels of the assertion about the community of women and children, which will provoke the interruption, Socrates insists on the continuous duration of the city once it has been properly founded: "And hence . . . the regime [πολιτεία], once well started, will roll on like a circle in its growth" (*Rep.* 424a). What is most curious about this assertion is that after the interruption—after the detour through philosophy—it will be retracted: lending his voice to the Muses, intoning their high tragic speech, Socrates will say, in their name, that not even a city so composed will remain for all time, that even it will be dissolved. That its dissolution may have to do with music, the gift of the Muses, is indicated by the anxious concern that Socrates expresses immediately after he has portrayed the city as a self-rolling circle: the overseers must guard against the corruption of the city by ensuring that there be "no innovation [νεωτερίζειν]² in gymnastic and music contrary to the established order [παρὰ τὴν τάξιν]" (*Rep.* 424b).

The primary declaration is itself divided, stating first the danger that results from the connection between music and politics, then affirming the benefit, the way in which music can be put in service to the city. In the first part Socrates declares: "For beware of change to a strange form of music [εἶδος γὰρ καινὸν μουσικῆς]³ as endangering the whole. For never are the tropes of music [μουσικῆς τρόποι] moved without the greatest political laws being moved, as Damon says, and I am persuaded" (*Rep.* 424c).⁴ Socrates draws a consequence, and then Adeimantus,

2. The word νεωτερίζειν means not only *to make innovations* but also to do so politically, that is, *to attempt political changes, to incite revolutionary movements.* Thus the semantics of the word already broaches the connection between music and politics that Socrates is about to declare.

3. The word καινόν means *new, newly introduced,* but its sense tends in a negative direction: *newfangled, strange.* In the *Apology* Socrates formulates the charge brought against him as that of believing in and teaching the youth about "other strange daimons" [ἕτερα . . . δαιμόνια καινά] (24b–c; 26b).

4. The basic sense of τρόπος is *turn, direction, way;* it also means, then, *manner* or *fashion,* and from this sense comes to designate *habit* or *custom* and thus a person's *character, temper,* or *disposition.* In music it means *mode* in the technical sense; the connection lies in the capacity of various musical modes to evoke corresponding dispositions in the soul.

Damon (born ca. 485 BC), to whose expertise Socrates appeals, was best known as a music theorist and teacher. But also he had an influential association with Pericles and taking up the discussion, adds an explanation of this declaration. The consequence: because of the danger that the introduction of strange forms of music may produce errant political changes, it is here in music, says Socrates, "that the guardians must build the guardhouse" (*Rep.* 424d). In particular, the guardhouse must be constructed in such a way as to keep musical lawlessness from creeping into the city, as it is wont to do, since it seems to be only harmless play. Adeimantus' account as to why it is not harmless serves to explain the general declaration regarding the politics of music: strange music, he says, "flows gently beneath the surface into the dispositions and practices [πρὸς τὰ ἤθη τε καὶ τὰ ἐπιτηδεύματα]." Thus shaping dispositions and orienting practices, it adversely affects the contracts that men make with one another and in this way launches an assault on the laws and the regime (πολιτεία), "until it finally subverts everything private and public" (*Rep.* 424d–e). The power of music to insinuate itself into the soul so as to shape its dispositions, thereby determining human practices, is what renders music politically effective and hence potentially dangerous.

Yet music can also provide protection from this very danger: what is required is that the youth engage only in "lawful play" and, in particular, that they be exposed only to the established, lawful music. Then, flowing into their souls, this lawfulness will accompany them in everything and will increase, "setting right anything in the city that may have previously been neglected" (*Rep.* 425a). Everything depends on the tropes, on their transposition into tropes of the soul. If they are right, the youth is set on the way to becoming a true guardian of the city,

Since naught so stockish, hard, and full of rage
But music for the time doth change his nature.

appears, in this and other connections, to have served as a private political advisor—hence the appropriateness of Socrates' reference to him in this passage on the connection between music and politics. For further details regarding Damon, see Debra Nails, *The People of Plato: A Prosopography of Plato and Other Socratics* (Indianapolis: Hackett, 2002), 121f.

If the tropes are not right or if the youth proves so unmusical as to be unreceptive, if he

> ... hath no music in himself,

then corruption will set in. In every instance the imperative is the same:

> Mark the music.

>>><<<

Music figured prominently in the life of the Greeks both public and private. At the Pythian Games there were musical contests right alongside the athletic events, and the winners of these contests were honored just as were the athletes. At the Panathenaea in Athens and the Carnea in Sparta, prizes were awarded for singing to the accompaniment of cithara or aulos. Such was in fact the most typical form of music in Greece. Lyric poetry was designed to be recited or sung to the accompaniment usually of a stringed instrument such as the cithara or lyre. Even Homer is said originally to have been recited in this manner. In the Homeric epics there are also portrayals of music being performed, sometimes in such a context as to allude to its connection with heroic action. Thus, in the *Iliad*, when the embassy from Agamemnon visits Achilles in his tent, they come upon him making music:

> They found Achilles taking joy in a lyre, clear-sounding,
> Splendid and carefully wrought, with a bridge of silver upon it,
> Which he won out of the spoils when he destroyed the city of Eëtion.
> With this he was taking joy and singing of men's fame.[5]

Greek music was predominantly melodic, choruses, for instance, usually singing in unison or in octaves. Though the instrumental accompaniment did not necessarily follow the melodic line, there

---

5. Homer, *Iliad* 9.186–89. The translation is adapted from that by Richard Lattimore: *The Iliad of Homer* (Chicago: University of Chicago Press, 1951).

seems to have been very little that was comparable to the counterpoint or complex harmonic structures of later music. Though there was indeed purely instrumental music, it seems to have been less common or at least to have been considered less significant; in Plato's *Laws* the Athenian declares that playing the aulos or cithara all alone—without singing—"must be regarded as unmusical virtuosity" (*Laws* 670a).

But music in all the forms it assumed in classical Greece (even where, as in Sparta, it was controlled) had in the *Republic* to be submitted to thoroughgoing critique. Within the project of the *Republic*, it is necessary, above all, to determine the form that music, in all its dimensions, must assume in order to instill in the souls of the guardians-to-be the dispositions conducive to proper leadership. It is only such music that is to be used in educating the future guardians.

Education in music comes first, even before gymnastic. This precedence is indicative of the power of music over the souls of the very young; indeed Socrates stresses that the very young are most pliable, most prone to assimilate themselves to whatever model is presented to them. Among the dimensions or elements of music, the first that Socrates addresses is the λόγος in music, which initially takes the form of μῦθοι, that is, of stories told to children, stories that are mostly false, though containing a bit of truth. One would expect Socrates to focus on the stories that are sung or at least recited with musical accompaniment; but Socrates' critique is at this point so completely focused on λόγος that its role even as an element specifically of music is temporarily set aside. Only later, once he has begun dealing with more exclusively musical elements such as melody, harmonic mode, and rhythm, does he return to consideration of λόγος specifically as an element within music and observe that such λόγος should follow the same strictures as λόγος that is not sung (see *Rep.* 398d). The way in which, in the discussion of the stories to be told to children, the interrogation of λόγος takes over, as it were, the entire field, virtually suspending consideration of anything musical, is indicative of just how significant the relation—or rather, a certain very special relation—between music and λόγος will prove to be.

Socrates does not hesitate to excoriate many of the stories currently told, stories deriving mostly from Homer and Hesiod, stories that misrepresent the gods and heroes, depicting the gods, for instance, as assuming manifold shapes and heroes as being overcome by their lamentings or wailings or by laughter. Along with the content of the stories, it is also necessary to supervise the style (λέξις), which should be of the mixed sort so as to preclude or at least not require imitation of characters who are unworthy. In addition to the content and style of the λόγος, music also includes the harmonic modes (ἁρμονία) and the rhythm (ῥυθμός), first of all as they pertain to the λόγος itself and then as they pertain to the melody and song (μέλος, ᾠδή).

At this point, where Socrates has just declared that they are finished with the part of music that concerns λόγος, Glaucon replaces Adeimantus as Socrates' interlocutor. Socrates himself will avow that he does not know the musical modes (ἁρμονία) (see *Rep.* 399a); but, addressing Glaucon with the declaration "You are musical," he will appeal to Glaucon's expertise. Yet, before turning to the particular modes, Socrates declares the main directive: the harmonic mode and the rhythm must follow the λόγος. Then the exclusion of wailing, already prescribed for the λόγος, is extended to the modes: the wailing modes, identified by Glaucon as Lydian, are to be excluded, kept outside the guardhouse of music that the guardians are to build. It is likewise with the modes that are soft and suitable for drinking parties, which Glaucon identifies as some Ionian and some Lydian. Those left are, he says, probably the Dorian and the Phrygian; when Socrates specifies that among the modes to be retained there should be one suitable to a man courageous in warlike deeds and another for a man who performs peaceful deeds, Glaucon confirms that these are precisely the ones he has just named.

Certain instruments are also to be excluded, because they are not needed for the modes retained. In particular, instruments that are many-stringed and play many modes are, along with the aulos, to be excluded, leaving, in the city at least, only the lyre and the cithara. As to rhythms, only those of an orderly and courageous life are to be retained, and they will be compelled, as will melody (μέλος), to follow the λόγος of such a man.

Socrates draws the discussion toward its conclusion by underlining why, in general, education in music is, as he says in the single word κυριωτάτη, most sovereign and most decisive. It is so, he explains, "because rhythm and harmony most of all insinuate themselves into the inmost part of the soul and most vigorously lay hold of it in bringing grace [εὐσχημοσύνη] with them" (*Rep.* 401d). He adds that whoever has been properly educated through rhythm and harmony will have the sharpest sense for what is—and what is not—a beautiful (καλός) product of τέχνη or of nature. Such a one would develop this sense while still young, "before," as Socrates says, "he is able to grasp λόγος. And when λόγος comes, the man who is reared in this way would take most delight in it, recognizing it on account of its being akin" (*Rep.* 402a).

This passage on the sovereignty and decisiveness of musical education is itself decisive. For now it is evident that musical education does not just shape the dispositions, producing thereby a tendency for certain kinds of practices or action. Rather, music of the proper kind sharpens our sense for what is beautiful so that when λόγος comes—not mere speech of any sort but speech that makes things manifest, that lets them shine, thus engendering the beautiful—we recognize and welcome it. What musical education instills is readiness for the reception of such λόγος.

It is this same connection that allows Socrates to mark the conclusion of their λόγος on music by saying that it has ended where it ought to end: for, he declares, "surely musical matters should end in love matters concerning the beautiful [εἰς τὰ τοῦ καλοῦ ἐρωτικά]" (*Rep.* 403c). His point is that musical education instills a sense for the beautiful and that the beautiful is precisely what is lovable; because education in music instills grace in the soul and opens its eyes, as it were, to the beautiful, its effect is to arouse ἔρως.

Socrates stipulates that what comes to be aroused is not to be an ἔρως that is mad (μανικός) or akin to excess (ἀκολασία); it is not to be at odds with the order and harmony of music nor with the grace they bestow on the soul; rather, it is to be an ἔρως carried out in a moderate and musical way (σωφρόνως τε καὶ μουσικῶς). And yet, one cannot but wonder whether ἔρως and moderation can be so conjoined or whether to ἔρως there does not always belong a certain madness and an inevitable excess.

This portion of the *Republic*, perhaps more than any other, needs to be read together with the *Phaedrus*, specifically with the portions of Socrates' second speech that have to do with ἔρως and with the beautiful. For the connection that in the *Republic* is delineated in the loose way appropriate to the context, namely, the connection between ἔρως, the beautiful, and the manifestness or shining forth of things, is, in the *Phaedrus*, set rigorously into a single expression: that the beautiful is the most shining forth and the most lovely [ὥστ' ἐκφανέστατον εἶναι καὶ ἐρασμιώτατον] (*Phaedr.* 250d–e). As to ἔρως as such, Socrates introduces it precisely as a form of the madness (μανία) sent by the gods (see *Phaedr.* 245b–c). And once he sets out to chart the course of erotic madness, he affirms the connection even more explicitly: "And when he that loves the beautiful is touched by such madness, he is called a lover" (*Phaedr.* 249d).[6]

At this point one begins to realize just how strategic the placement of the entire discussion of music in the *Republic* really is. For throughout this part of the *Republic* there operates—as can be shown[7]—a certain abstraction from a dimension of human life that includes ἔρως along with mating, procreation, birth, sexual difference, and corporeal singularity. It is this abstraction that sets the stage for the comedy that erupts in Book 5 and that leads eventually to a philosophical plane where the human phenomena previously passed over can be brought into the discussion. Because of this overall dynamic structure, the discussion of

6. See *Being and Logos*, 132–35; 153–59.
7. See ibid., 355–59; 372–78; see also *Chorology*, 24–27.

music as carried out in Books 3 and 4 is limited. It can, at most, merely broach consideration of ἔρως and of the beautiful; within this limited perspective, determined precisely by the abstraction from the erotic, ἔρως itself cannot but appear as moderate or at least as capable of moderation, not to say domestication.

A deferral will therefore prove to operate in Socrates' conclusion that musicality should end in erotics of the beautiful. For the erotics to which music will eventually lead, in which it will decisively reach its end, will concern an ἔρως that reaches far beyond the present dimension, an ἔρως not sheltered from madness and excess, an ἔρως that, drawn by the beautiful, opens upon being as such.

>>><<<

For all the stress put on the role of music in education, Socrates acknowledges that there is also a danger of too much music, especially if it is of a kind other than those that he and Glaucon have specified. If a man gives himself over and lets the sweet, soft, wailing songs of the aulos pour into his ears as into a funnel, he begins to melt away; his spirited part (θυμός) becomes liquefied and finally dissolves completely. The response that Socrates proposes to this danger is not only to exclude the modes and other elements of music that further this dissolution but also to pair musical education with gymnastic education. Whereas at the outset Socrates took for granted the common assumption that music is for the soul and gymnastic for the body, he now insists—without denying the effect of gymnastic on the body—that both music and gymnastic are for the soul: music for the philosophic nature or what Socrates will later call the calculating part (λογιστικόν), gymnastic for the spirited part (θυμός). By harmonizing these two natures, the philosophic and the spirited—so at another level submitting them to music—a man is, according to Socrates, made both moderate and courageous (see *Rep.* 410c–e; also 441e). The man who makes the finest mixture of music and gymnastic and brings them to bear on his soul in proper measure, thereby harmonizing his two natures, practicing a kind of music of the soul, is, according to Socrates, most correctly said to be the most musical. Yet even the music of this most musical man, elevated above the music of sounds in order to harmonize the effect of such music with that of gymnastic, still—as we shall see—falls short of the genuinely higher music.

Consideration of music and gymnastic is resumed in Book 7, in the reiteration of the story of the cave that is devoted specifically to setting out the course of the education of the guardians. Since the guiding aim of education is to turn the soul around into the ascent to being, that is, to draw it upward into philosophy, the question that must be addressed at the outset is whether the means already prescribed for the early education of the guardians, namely, music and gymnastic, suffice for—or at least contribute to—directing the soul upward toward being. When Socrates poses this question, Glaucon recalls that music was found to educate the guardians by transmitting to them a certain harmoniousness, but not knowledge (οὐκ ἐπιστήμην). In music and its effect, he adds conclusively, there is not to be found a learning (μάθημα) directed toward what is now sought (see *Rep.* 522a–b).

Proceeding from this conclusion, Socrates then goes on to set out the curriculum that the guardians will be required to follow: the sequence of five mathematical disciplines followed by dialectic. Too much emphasis should not be placed, however, on the discontinuity between the earlier education in music and gymnastic and the advanced education in mathematics and dialectic. For it has been noted that, by sharpening the sense of the beautiful, musical education has the effect of instilling in the soul a certain receptiveness to λόγος. Thus, musical education produces in the soul a readiness to receive not only the rigorous λόγοι that would constitute dialectic but also the more rudimentary λόγοι—ratios, for instance, which is one of the senses of the word—that are involved in the mathematical disciplines.

Granted the limitation of music, granted that it is, at best, only preparatory for the philosophical ascent, there are nonetheless, as

Eva Brann has emphasized,[8] significant indications that there is yet another music, a higher music, philosophical music, the music that in the *Phaedo* Socrates calls the "greatest music" (*Phaedo* 61a), identifying it with philosophy itself and distinguishing it from ordinary, demotic music. Brann mentions Socrates' remark, following the exposition of the mathematical curriculum, that the entire preceding course is only "a prelude to the song itself [προοίμια ἐστιν αὐτοῦ τοῦ νόμου]" (*Rep.* 531d). She mentions also the remark, shortly thereafter, that at this point it is a matter of "the song itself that dialectic performs [αὐτός ἐστιν ὁ νόμος ὃν τὸ διαλέγεσθαι περαίνει]" (*Rep.* 532a). To be sure, the polysemy of all the key words involved here is such that one could select their meaning (and so translate the remarks) so as to avoid in both instances any reference to music.[9] Yet it seems much more likely that Plato is playing on the entire semantic register, stretching these portions of text, as it were, between multiple senses, making them hover between different semantic values. In this case a more structural conception might well be more appropriate than simply identifying here a doubling of music at the higher level. Then one might say that demotic music is somehow transposed (in the literal and the musical sense) into a higher music, that, in the philosophical ascent to being, music as such—and not just metaphorically—remains somehow operative. Then, as Socrates said earlier, musicality would prove to end in erotics, but now an erotics no longer subject to the repression that haunted the earlier discussion. For this higher music, this music transposed to the plane of dialectic, would be the sounding of an ἔρως irremediably excessive in its directedness to being and beyond.

8. Eva Brann, *The Music of the Republic* (Philadelphia: Paul Dry Books, 2004), 153–58.

9. The word προοίμιον means, in music, *prelude, overture;* in speeches, *preface, exordium;* in reference to laws, *preamble;* metaphorically, any *beginning.* The word νόμος means *custom, convention; law; song, ode.* The meaning of περαίνω is not only *perform, bring about* but also *bring to an end, complete.* Among the possible permutations some would refer specifically to law, some to speech, some to music, and, in each case, as something either to bring about or bring to an end. Others would be mixed or generalized.

What, then, about the politics of music? If the reference is to this higher music, to the song that dialectic performs, then the relation to politics is none other than that of philosophy itself to politics. In a sense the entire *Republic* revolves around the paradoxy of this relation, the paradoxy that consists in the necessity both of conjunction and of disconnection. The philosopher must be ruler and yet must be forced, must force himself, to forsake his vision and return to the cave. In Book 7 this paradoxy is played out precisely in the exposition of the guardians' curriculum. Since in the figure of the guardian there is to be embodied the conjunction of philosopher and of warrior or ruler, Socrates insists at the outset that each discipline in the curriculum must both serve to turn the soul toward being and also be useful to warlike men. Indeed such proves to be the case with the first such discipline: arithmetic is needed both because it focuses thought on the ones that are to be posited so as to resolve the mixing up of opposites that we perceive *and also* because it enables the leader to put his army in order. Yet already at the level of arithmetic the discussion is devoted almost entirely to the philosophical use, and as Socrates and Glaucon move on through the ever higher disciplines, their use for the guardians as protectors of the city receives less and less attention; finally, in connection with harmonics and then dialectic, it is not mentioned at all. In effect, this discussion enacts the separation between the needs of the guardians and those of the philosopher, that is, the disconnection between politics and the higher, philosophical music. Nothing highlights this disconnection more dramatically than the outcome of Book 7, in which it is prescribed that in order to bring about the city that has been built in λόγος all who are older than ten will be expelled, so that there remains then a city consisting only of philosophers and children. In other words, the philosopher proves so thoroughly disconnected from the city that the effect of his presence is to expel the city from itself.

It is otherwise with the politics of demotic music. Regardless of whether and how the philosopher is related to the city, the saying of Damon will remain valid for demotic music and pertinent to the city: change in the tropes of music will produce change in the laws, and change to strange forms of music will have pernicious political consequences. For, as Socrates has explained, music shapes disposition and lawless dispositions have, in turn, ruinous effects on the contracts that regulate dealings among men; the ruin of contractual arrangements eventually subverts both law and regime.

However, when in Book 8 Socrates turns—or returns—to the discussion of the decline of the city, the emphasis is not on the ruinous effect of strange music but on the gradual loss of musical sense as the decline sets in. The inception of decline has to do with calculation—or rather, miscalculation—of the nuptial number. And though a kind of higher, mathematical music enters into this calculation (Socrates mentions specifically the production of two harmonies), the loss of musical sense begins to appear with the first generation of those who, because of the ignorance of the previous generation regarding the number and hence regarding the proper times for begetting, are conceived out of season. These untimely conceived guardians become negligent, giving less consideration to music and to gymnastic, so that their children, in turn, become more unmusical. Hence, the very first signs of the decline of the city are neglect of music and loss of musicality (see *Rep.* 546d). In light of the earlier discussion, it is clear that this loss will curtail the proper forming of the soul and, in particular, the sharpening of the sense of the beautiful that readies the soul for the reception of λόγος. Becoming more unmusical entails also becoming less fluent in speech.

With the transition to timocracy, the first in the series of progressively worse regimes, music again suffers neglect. Because in this regime honor and courage are most respected, gymnastic is given priority over music; there is, as Socrates says, "neglect of the true Muse accompanied by λόγοι and philosophy" (*Rep.* 548b), that is, neglect of music in every sense. The timocratic man, with his heightened spiritedness, will have lost somewhat—though not entirely—his sense for music. Socrates says—comparing him to Glaucon—that such a man is "somewhat less apt at music, although he is friendly toward it [φιλόμουσος]" (*Rep.* 548e). Since music fosters speech, the timocratic man is, as Socrates observes, less skilled in speaking; he does not base his claim to rule on speaking, on his capacity for λόγος, but on warlike deeds. He delights, not in music and speech, but in gymnastic and the hunt. He is one who, says Socrates, has been "abandoned by the best guardian"—namely, as Socrates answers in response to Adeimantus, who replaces the musical Glaucon at just this point: "λόγος mixed with music" (*Rep.* 549b).

Socrates continues to trace the decline of the city, from timocracy to oligarchy, to democracy, to tyranny. Yet, most remarkably, there is no mention whatsoever of music in the entire remainder of this discourse. Presumably, one is to conclude that the abandonment that the timocratic man suffers is definitive and that in those more dissolute forms that the city and man assume music's salutary formative power no longer plays a role.

And yet, if, in the more dissolute regimes, music no longer shapes the soul's receptiveness to beauty and to λόγος, does it, in some strange way, contribute to bringing about the dissolution? For, as Damon says and Socrates is persuaded, change to a strange form of music is a danger to the city as a whole.

>>><<<

On the question of such musical dissolution the *Republic* remains completely silent. It is only in the *Laws* that this question is taken up. In order to address this aspect of the politics of music, it is thus necessary to turn to the *Laws*, to read a passage from this dialogue together with those already considered from the *Republic*.

Yet, as in every case, reading two dialogues together, even, as here, in sequence, requires being attentive to their heterogeneity. Thus it is necessary to mark, in particular, the difference in voice and setting: in the *Laws* most of what is said is voiced by one designated merely as an Athenian; also, set in Crete on the road from Knossos to the cave and the temple of Zeus, the discussion has an ambiance and an orientation quite different from those of the conversation pursued by Socrates in the house of Polemarchus in the Piraeus. Furthermore, the ordering of a political regime (πολιτεία) takes on, in the *Laws*, a second part that is almost entirely lacking in the *Republic*. The Athenian in fact draws the distinction between the two parts (see *Laws* 751a–b). There is, first, the institution of the rulers and of the manner in which they should be chosen; this part is shared by the two dialogues. The second part, carried out in the *Laws* but not in the *Republic*, consists in setting up a code of laws for the rulers to administer. Also in the *Laws* the Athenian distinguishes clearly between the kind of constitution (πολιτεία) that the *Republic* sets up ("no one will ever set down a more correct or better definition than this of what constitutes the extreme as regards virtue—such a city . . . inhabited, presumably, by gods or children of gods" [*Laws* 739d]) and that which is established in the *Laws*, a regime that, if it came into being (as, presumably, that of the *Republic* could not), would be "the nearest to immortality and second in point of honor" (*Laws* 739e).[10] This difference is reflected in the otherwise astonishing fact that the word *philosophy* does not occur at all in the *Laws*.

To a certain extent, however, the difference of context in the two dialogues is mitigated when the theme is not the best city but rather those that belong to the series of ever more dissolute regimes. Indeed there are close correspondences between the respective discussions of these kinds of cities, though, because their perspectives are different, the *Laws* regards the regimes more affirmatively, whereas the *Republic* regards them only in terms of their decline from the best regime. Yet even this difference is mitigated in the case of the passage in the *Laws* on musical dissolution, for the Athenian has nothing affirmative to say about the lawless democracy that, he contends, is the consequence of a certain lawlessness in music.

The Athenian introduces his account by way of a story, a brief history of the period when the Greeks were attacked by the

10. Brann suggests that the constitution developed in the *Laws* is meant "as a practical political model for actual cities" (*The Music of the Republic*, 148).

Persians. At that time, he reports, the Athenians had an ancient regime or constitution (πολιτεία) that involved certain rulers based on a division into four classes. He continues, speaking mostly in first-person: there was also a sense of shame or honor (αἰδώς), which, like a despotic mistress, made us willing to live as slaves to the laws then existing. The threat posed by the Persians bound us, he continues, more firmly to our laws and rulers. Also, he says, as he recounts the battle of Marathon and other engagements, we Athenians were bound more closely in friendship to each other, this bond being the result of our fear (φόβος), our fear of defeat by the Persians and the fear that consisted in the sense of shame inculcated by our enslavement to the laws. Without this fear, he says, the Athenians would never have united in self-defense and saved themselves.

Against the background of this story, the Athenian then sets out to explain, as he puts it, "the origin of the excessive development of the free way of life" (*Laws* 700a). At the time about which he has just been speaking, there were firm laws regulating music. They dictated the division of music in accord with its own forms and figures. There was one form that consisted in prayers to the gods, and these were called *hymns*; there was another form that concerned the birth of Dionysus, and these were called *dithyrambs*—and so on. It was not allowed to misuse one form of song for another. Also, music was judged, not by the clapping and whistling of the unmusical mob, but by the educated, who listened to the end in silence.

But then, after a time, there appeared poets who were ignorant of music, and they instigated unmusical lawlessness in music. They jumbled everything together, mixing hymns with dithyrambs, using the sound of the cithara to imitate the sound of the aulos, and so on. They even went so far as to assert that there was no such thing as correct music, thus falsifying music itself and leaving nothing but pleasure as the criterion for judging it. In this way, the ignorant poets instilled in many a lawlessness regarding music and made them think that they too could judge the excellence of music. The Athenian says: "in place of an aristocracy in music, a wretched theatocracy has emerged" (*Laws* 701a)—or rather, a democracy. Yet, he continues, if only a democracy *in music* had arisen, the outcome would not have been so bad. But from this change regarding music, there arose the opinion that everyone is wise in everything. Together with this lawlessness, people became fearless and shameless. Such freedom engendered, in turn, the loss of willingness to be governed by rulers, then rejection of governance by parents and elders. Next, they sought not to have to obey laws at all—indeed not even to be subject to laws. Then, finally, says the Athenian, comes the ultimate freedom (ἐλευθερία): "they cease to give heed at all to oaths and pledges and to everything pertaining to the gods" (*Laws* 701c). A harsh, lawless epoch comes to prevail.

Such is, then, the politics of music. Such is the power of music to transform a regime and a city. When music becomes lawless, when the very order that it would instill in the soul and hence in the city dissolves into disorder and utter disregard for its proper forms, the result is lawless democracy. More precisely, what lawlessness in music produces is not just a democratic city, not just a city with a democratic regime. Rather, what it produces is the lawlessness that, at the very core of democracy, renders democracy eminently dangerous, whatever might in other regards be said in its behalf. What lawlessness in music produces is a freedom or license that consists in the transgression of law, in the dissolution of civil order (παρανομία), and in the dominance of the belief that all are equally knowing, equally imbued with wisdom.

As, finally, swept up in the spread of lawlessness, its spread from music throughout the city at large, men cease to heed even the difference that sets the gods apart from them, they slip back toward a pre-Olympian state of harshness and evil. As the Athenian says, they come "to imitate the nature of the Titans of old," reverting to such a nature, coming to display it in themselves. Thus it is, as he says, that "they spend their lives in a harsh epoch in which there is never a cessation of evils" (*Laws* 701c).

>>><<<

For the Greeks the figure of Orpheus inscribes mythically both the power of music, its economy, and a corresponding politics of music. All are in play when Orpheus makes a brief appearance in the story of Er at the end of the *Republic* (620a). The scene, observed by Er, is one in which several souls are choosing the life that they are about to begin living. For the most part, they make their choice according to the habits or happenings of their previous life. The soul that once belonged to Orpheus is no exception. Because of his previous death at the hands of Maenads, his resolve is not to be reborn of woman. He chooses the life of a swan, reconfirming in the choice of this "musical animal," as it is called, his own musicality.

The mythical figure portrays Orpheus as one who sang and played the lyre, producing music so clear and ringing that it could arouse the utmost zeal or calm the angriest of spirits. His music was of such beauty that it once rendered even the Sirens inaudible, delivering Jason and his crew from the danger. Yet the stories tell, above all, of the events that ensued when, immediately after their wedding, his bride Eurydice was stung by a viper and died. Orpheus resolved to descend to Hades to bring Eurydice back, and it was the power of his music that allowed him to do so. With his lyre he charmed Cerberus, who guarded the gates of Hades, and so he was allowed to enter. Then his music gave such delight to Persephone and Pluto himself that they could not refuse him what he asked. Under the spell of his music, they summoned Eurydice and delivered her to him, but with the condition that as she followed him up out of Hades he was not to look back at her until they had reached the upper world. Though, as he then ascended, he longed to cast a glance back to assure himself that she was indeed following, he resisted until he had completed the ascent. Only when he finally stepped out into the daylight did he cast his glance back toward her. Yet the right moment had not yet come, for she was still within the passageway. He saw her in the dim light and held out his arm to her, but at that moment she was gone. Eurydice had slipped back into the darkness, and from her came only the one faint word "farewell."

In the myth, as at the beginning of the *Republic*, there is a descent into Hades, a κατάβασις. There is also, as with the Socratic λόγοι, an attempt at return from the underworld. At the center of the *Republic* this mythic figure, its directionality, is inverted in the figure of ascent from the cave and descent to which the philosopher-guardian is compelled. Yet the figure is not free of blind spots, of discontinuities where one knows not how a transition has occurred, nor what may, in such an interval, have intervened. At the end of the *Republic,* which corresponds in deed to the initial descent to Piraeus/Hades, Er returns to life; but when he does so, the one thing he does not know is how he came back into his body. Something about the ascent remains enigmatic, something about the moment when it would finally be completed, the moment when the escaped prisoner would finally come to look upon the sun itself, the moment when Orpheus steps out into the sunlight and casts his glance back at Eurydice disappearing into the darkness. It is a moment in which one recognizes the futility of calling upon music or λόγος in hopes of securing presence. It is a moment in which there prevails only the vision of withdrawal.

The figure of Orpheus has never ceased being celebrated, depicted in word and image, and set to music. Celebrated in tragedy by Aeschylus and Euripides for the power that his music has to charm wild beasts and even trees and stones, he was often the subject also of Attic vase-painting; a scene depicting him in the underworld is attributed to Polygnotus, often considered the first great Greek painter. Musical settings, musical celebrations of his music, are abundant, from the operas of Monteverdi and Gluck to the 1858 opéra bouffe, *Orphée aux enfers* by Jacques Offenbach. One of Liszt's most acclaimed symphonic poems is a musical depiction of Orpheus' descent to and ascent from Hades. The name *Orpheus* became virtually the proper name of music itself, to such an extent that when, in 1698, Henry Purcell published a collection of his own vocal solos, duets, and trios, he entitled the collection *Orpheus Britannicus.*

Orpheus is also the theme of a text by Maurice Blanchot. This text, "The Gaze of Orpheus,"[11] begins with a declaration

---

11. Maurice Blanchot, "Le Regard d'Orphée," in *L'Espace littéraire* (Paris: Gallimard, 1955), 227–34. The passages cited from this text are taken from the first two pages.

of the power and politics of music: "When Orpheus descends
to Eurydice, art is the power that causes the night to open."
What counts in Blanchot's reading is less the power to draw near
Eurydice than the capacity that music provides for experiencing
the night, the depths. It is through art—specifically, through
music, to keep to the figure of Orpheus—that one is enabled
to touch upon the obscure depths, to encounter this night. On
the other hand, these depths do not themselves open up, open
out, into the light. Hades is closed, sealed off, a realm of shades
shut away in darkness. This night is a night that does not pass
into day, a night that never becomes day. It is, in Blanchot's
expression, the other night (*l'autre nuit*). As a name covering this
night, Eurydice marks the limit that art—preeminently music—
can attain: "concealed behind a name and covered by a veil, she
is the profoundly dark point toward which art, desire, death,
and the night all seem to lead. She is the instant in which the
essence of the night approaches as the *other* night." Naming the
darkness, Eurydice in Hades marks the radical concealment that
is the limit of art and of life (in relation both to desire and
to death). In this connection, limit means that toward which art
and life have an essential orientation, that which serves to delimit
them, but which they cannot master, cannot appropriate, cannot
make fully their own, banning every alterity.

Yet Orpheus is not set simply on encountering the darkness. In
Blanchot's words: "His *work* is to bring it back into the daylight
and in the daylight give it form, figure, and reality." In other
words, he descends into the night in order then to draw it up
into the daylight into which it does *not*, of itself, enter. Drawing
it into the daylight requires giving to the formless shade of Hades
a certain form, figure, and reality, almost as if it could be one
of those things upon the earth that shine forth in the light that
fills the open sky. And yet, it is *not* one of these things to be
beheld in its shining, and he can draw it up into the light only
by keeping his back turned to it. Blanchot writes: "Orpheus can
do anything except look this 'point' in the face, look at the center
of the night in the night. . . . He can draw it upwards, but only

by keeping his back turned to it. This turning away is the only way he can approach it: this is the meaning of the concealment [*le sens de la dissimulation*] revealed in the night." In other words, he must bring it into the daylight in such a way as also to let it remain concealment; he must draw it up into the open in a way that also lets it remain closed in the depths. In still other words, the depth, the night, does not submit to the gaze, which would divest it of its very character as concealment. If it is to be revealed, it must be revealed as concealed. Blanchot avers that this occurs in the artwork: "it only reveals itself by concealing itself in the work."

Yet it is the step beyond this that is most exorbitant of all, a step in the direction of a kind of exorbitancy. Let us read further: "But the myth also shows that Orpheus' destiny is not to submit to that law—and it is certainly true that by turning around to look at Eurydice, Orpheus ruins the work . . . , and Eurydice returns to the shadows. . . . But if he did not turn around to look at Eurydice, he still would be betraying, being disloyal to, the boundless and imprudent force of his impulse, which does not demand Eurydice in her diurnal truth and her everyday charm, but in her nocturnal darkness, in her distance, her body closed, her face sealed, which wants to see her not when she is visible, but when she is invisible, and not as the intimacy of a familiar life, but as the strangeness of that which excludes all intimacy; it does not want to make her live, but to have the fullness of her death living in her. . . . This is an infinitely problematic impulse which the day condemns as an unjustifiable act of madness or as the expiation of excess."

Here there is interruption. Unwilling, out of madness or excess, to leave the depth concealed in the work, the musician opens his ears to other tones, to wild, dissonant tones, and the philosopher lets his λόγοι collide with what would be concealment as such, were such concealment not the very undoing of the *as such* as such.

There is also said to be music of the heaven, its beautiful harmony matching the magnificent order that vision apprehends

in the starry heaven. In *The Merchant of Venice*, Lorenzo attests
to both when he says to Jessica:

> Look how the floor of heaven
> Is thick inlaid with patens of bright gold.
> There's not the smallest orb which thou behold'st
> But in his motion like an angel sings,
> Still quiring to the young-eyed cherubins;
> Such harmony is in immortal souls,
> But whilst this muddy vesture of decay
> Doth grossly close it in, we cannot hear it.
>
> (V.i.58–65)

The speech poetizes a gesture that goes back to the *Timaeus*.
Yet in the *Timaeus* there is a difference, and everything hinges
on this difference. The relevant passage comes at the end of
Timaeus' first discourse on the cosmos. In this discourse in which
Timaeus tells how the god constructed the cosmos, he emphasizes the order and harmony that go into it, detailing how this
work of νοῦς, as he calls it, is made to permeate the soul of the
cosmos. On the other hand, the elements (fire, air, water, earth)
that go to make up the body of the cosmos, though brought into
the account, are simply taken for granted as such. They are there
in the work of the god and in the discourse of the philosopher,
yet only as concealed with regard to their proper composition.

It is at the end of this cosmological discourse that Timaeus
turns to the heaven and observes that the orderly revolutions to
be beheld there are given to us that we might, in turn, instill such
order in our souls, imitating within ourselves the revolutions seen
in the heaven. Then he pairs this observation with an analogous
one about music. The harmonies of music, like the order of the
heaven, are given us by the Muses that we might instill them, by
imitation, in ourselves (see *Tim.* 46e–47e).[12]

One can readily imagine that as Timaeus voices these obser-
vations he raises his eyes to the heaven where this order is to be
seen. And one can readily imagine him imagining that he hears

12. See *Chorology*, 89–90.

not only the harmonious sounds of cithara and aulos but also the inaudible harmonies of the heaven. Then it would be all the more striking that at just this point in the discourse a dissonance begins to be heard, the distant sounding of the elements that are not the work of νοῦς and that, concealed within the work, cannot but disturb the order and harmony toward which the ascensional vision is drawn.

This is the moment of interruption, the moment when Timaeus actually breaks off his discourse in order to begin anew. It is also the moment when he begins to turn toward what lies concealed in the work, to what is revealed there only as concealed. It is the moment when the madness and excess that will haunt, if not animate, the chorology first erupt. It is the moment when Orpheus turns to look back, to look directly, at Eurydice. Once this turn has been made, music and λόγος will never again be the same.

5

On the Verge

The thinking enacted in *Contributions to Philosophy* is set out in the wake of nihilism. It must already have come to tell the story of how the true world finally became a fable; and, twisting free of the now fabulous true world, this thinking ventures a new beginning apart from the Platonic distinction of intelligible and sensible that framed the story of the history of metaphysics; it ventures a beginning on the verge. Thus set apart from the very determinants of nihilism, most notably from the now vacuous conceptual resources required even to determine nihilism as the utter lack of goals, thinking would press on toward a more originary happening. Thus, in *Contributions to Philosophy* Heidegger writes: "The abandonment of Being is the ground and thus also the more originary essential determination of that which Nietzsche recognized for the first time as nihilism" (*BP* §57).

And yet, precisely as thinking presses on, venturing to engage in the crossing to another beginning, it cannot but be drawn back to an implication attached to nihilism. This implication is sounded in the most penetrating tones in Nietzsche's discourse on the madman. Yet one needs to dispel the aura of familiarity that this passage in *The Gay Science* has acquired. One needs to hear, again and yet almost as if for the first time, the words with which the madman, amongst those in the marketplace, proclaimed the death of God—or rather, since those in the marketplace mostly did not believe in God, the words with which he declared the frightful implications of this event. All the implications converge in the title that functions as his name. These implications are cast as questions, as impossible questions that nonetheless make unmistakable the dire consequences now in store. The madman poses, for instance, the question "Who gave us the sponge to wipe away the entire horizon?"[1]—poses the question in order to declare, in all its strangeness, the utter absence of horizon. To have no horizon whatsoever so as, in his words, to stray "as through an infinite nothing" can only imply being thrown into madness. "Is not night and more night coming on all the while?" asks the madman, perpetual night without any promise of dawn, *l'autre nuit,* in Blanchot's phrase. Lighting a lantern in the bright morning hours, one will seem deranged, will appear to have succumbed to madness, may indeed have become mad.

Heidegger is not oblivious to the implication nor to Nietzsche's own entrapment in it. Near the end of his lecture course *The Will to Power as Art,* which is from the same period as *Contributions to Philosophy,* he writes: "During the time when the overturning of Platonism became for Nietzsche a twisting free of it, madness befell him."[2] In *Contributions to Philosophy* not only Nietzsche but also Hölderlin—who perhaps even more insistently let a lantern be lit in the bright morning hours—is said to have "suffered most profoundly the uprooting to which Western history is driven." As if, as Hölderlin says of Oedipus, they had an eye too many, these—in Heidegger's words—"had to depart from the brightness of their days prematurely" (*BP* §105).

Nothing is more seriously threatened by nihilism than speech. For throughout the history of metaphysics what has always served to secure speech, to stabilize and guarantee its meaning, is the

---

1. Friedrich Nietzsche, *Die fröhliche Wissenschaft,* in vol. V2 of *Werke: Kritische Gesamtausgabe,* ed. Giorgio Colli and Mazzino Montinari (Berlin: de Gruyter, 1973), §125.

2. Heidegger, *Nietzsche* (Pfullingen: Günther Neske, 1961), 233.

intelligible. As long as a true world (in Nietzsche's phrase), a domain of pure significations, was taken to be established anterior to speech, speech had only to express in the sensible sign a chain of meanings absolutely precedent to all acts of speech. Even if the relation of sign to meaning, of signifier to signified, was purely conventional, the meaningfulness of speech, the possibility and stability of meaning, was guaranteed in advance. But with the advent of nihilism, once the true world finally became a fable, this guarantee of meaning disappears. Nietzsche's inversion of Platonism confirms that the entire horizon of intelligibility has been wiped away so that one no longer knows what speech signifies, no longer knows even what it means for speech to signify, to be meaningful. Once one takes the further step and twists free of the very schema of intelligible and sensible, everything about speech is set adrift; even if there remain certain concrete attestations to the possibility of meaningful speech, one is left entirely at a loss as to how this possibility could be thought, as to how it could itself be said. As nihilism proves to be grounded in the abandonment of being, even the word *being* is threatened with the prospect of becoming, as Nietzsche says, only a fallacy and a vapor, "the last smoke of evaporating reality."[3]

Or rather, what is said, since both write in German, is that the word *Sein* is threatened with this prospect. In marking this difference, I want to impede the tendency—which I have not hindered up to this point—to let the German words and phrases cited from Nietzsche and Heidegger slip all too readily into corresponding English words and phrases. Such impediment is imperative, above all, in the wake of nihilism; for if speech as such is destabilized by the abandonment of anterior intelligibility, translation is no less thrown into question. In the classical determination translation turns precisely on the anterior signification, moving from its expression in one language to the expression of the same meaning in another language. Once it can no longer be hinged to anterior signification, translation becomes a different

---

3. Nietzsche, *Götzen-Dämmerung*, in vol. VI3 of *Werke*, 70.

kind of task, inseparable from interpretation and no doubt from other operations that have still to be thoroughly analyzed. The task is compounded in the case of a text such as *Contributions to Philosophy* that is openly exposed to the impact of the destabilization of language and translation. Any discourse on Heidegger's text will, with only scant resources, have to contend at every turn with translation and with the question of translation.

Set out in the wake of nihilism, the thinking ventured in *Contributions to Philosophy* is exposed both to the utter insecurity of speech and to the threat—if it be only a threat—of madness. The inscription assumes as the very outset an orientation to speech, namely, to the title of the text and to the linguistic insecurity reflected in the title. Heidegger begins: "The public title must now necessarily sound bland, ordinary, as though saying nothing" (*BP*, initial, unnumbered section). The blandness of the title *Beiträge zur Philosophie* is reproduced in the English *Contributions to Philosophy*. Yet this blandness corresponds to a necessity, not in the sense of the traditional modal category, but in a sense newly determined—or rather, in the process of being determined—in Heidegger's text: necessity (*Notwendigkeit*) as a turning (*Wenden*) from out of need or distress (*Not*). As he continues, Heidegger identifies this need or distress as constituted by the present insecurity of speech: "Philosophy cannot be publicly announced otherwise, because all essential titles have become impossible since all fundamental words have been used up and the genuine relation to the word has been destroyed." The fundamental words that have been used up are primarily those that provided the resources for the great modern treatises of metaphysics, words that are for the most part translations or even transliterations of the Latin renderings of the basic Greek philosophical words. Heidegger insists that the using up of fundamental words began indeed with the Latin translation of the fundamental words of Greek philosophy—for instance, of ἐνέργεια as *actualitas* and of φύσις as *natura*—and that this initial phase was the most decisive of all. Like coins left in circulation so long that the inscription on them is finally effaced, so the words with which the Greek thinkers had thought and said *Being* lost their force to the point where finally they could say virtually everything and therefore nothing. Even *Being and Time,* for all its linguistic innovation, continued in significant respects to draw on these words, securing them to some degree by reference back to classical texts. And yet, the exhaustion of this language proved to be a major obstacle to carrying out the turn by which the project of *Being and Time* would have been completed. Referring to the projected, never published Third Division "Time and Being," Heidegger writes, many years later: "The Division in question was held back because thinking failed in the adequate saying of this turning and did not succeed with the help of the language of metaphysics."[4] The exhaustion of the language of metaphysics reaches its extreme when, with the advent of nihilism, the metaphysics of language undergoes, together with metaphysics as such, its inversion and displacement. There is no more direct—or more abysmal— attestation than that of Nietzsche: "It is this way with all of us concerning language: we believe that we know something about the things themselves when we speak of trees, colors, snow, and flowers; and yet we possess nothing but metaphors for things— metaphors that correspond in no way to the original entities."[5]

The exhaustion of language is no doubt a factor in Heidegger's insistence that *Contributions to Philosophy* can venture only an attempt (*nur ein Versuch*) and that, as he says, it "must avoid all false claim to be a 'work' of the style hitherto" (*BP,* initial, unnumbered section). Yet what kind of text can such a venture produce? What kind of text is still possible now that all fundamental words have been used up? Must new coins be minted, new fundamental words somehow forged? One might well suppose that certain apt words are to be reendowed with sense. And yet, now, lacking recourse to an anterior intelligibility, one scarcely knows how even the sense of such reendowment could be determined.

4. Heidegger, *Brief über den "Humanismus"* (1946), in *Wegmarken,* vol. 9 of *Gesamtausgabe,* 328.

5. Nietzsche, *Über Wahrheit und Lüge im aussermoralischen Sinne,* in vol. III2 of *Werke,* 373.

What can be written now that the genuine relation to the word has been destroyed? Must this relation not be restored in some measure in order for even a mere venture to be possible? To restore the genuine relation to words is to draw speech back into proximity to what is to be said in such a way that saying becomes disclosive. In the wake of nihilism, which is grounded in the abandonment of Being, what needs above all to be genuinely said is Being. How, then, is speech—the speech of thinking, thoughtful speech—to be drawn back into proximity to Being? How could speech be thus drawn otherwise than as speech, otherwise than in and through speaking? The venture begins therefore with the thoughtful saying of that which prompts a renewed saying of Being, of that which draws speech back into proximity to Being and makes its words the words of Being. This beginning, this thoughtful saying, is enacted in the final sentence of the initial, unnumbered section of Heidegger's text: "*Vom Ereignis er-eignet ein denkerisch-sagendes Zugehören zum Seyn und in das Wort 'des' Seyns.*"

Considering that Heidegger later writes that *Ereignis* "can no more be translated than the Greek λόγος or the Chinese Tao,"[6] this passage must be declared in some measure untranslatable. While indeed granting this untranslatability, I will nonetheless press toward translating, for it is precisely in experiencing the resistance to translation that one is impelled to think what is said in *Ereignis* and to gather around it a discourse that, in another sense, does translate it, regardless of whether this discourse is cast in German, in English, or in Chinese.

This beginning offers little more than the word. Even the effecting that proceeds from or by what is thus named is identified only through a doubling of the word: *Vom Ereignis er-eignet.* . . . It should be noted, too, that the beginning made with this word will eventually lead around to a manifold interrogation of beginning as such; for the very directionality of Heidegger's venture in

---

6. Heidegger, *Identität und Differenz* (Pfullingen: Günther Neske, 1957), 29.

Contributions to Philosophy is determined by the difference and play between two beginnings.

But in this beginning passage the decisive connection is that of *Ereignis* to that which proceeds from or by it, that which could be called, in the strict sense, the issue of *Ereignis*. According to the passage the issue of *Ereignis* is—venturing now to translate: "a belonging of thoughtful saying to Beyng and to the word 'of' Beyng." The issue of *Ereignis* is to draw thoughtful saying into proximity to Being so that its words become those of Being.

Proximity denotes nonseparation, belonging. Thus the discourse is not merely about something; it does not represent something simply apart from the discourse. The thoughtful saying does not describe or explain anything; for, as Heidegger writes, "here the saying is not over against what is to be said but is this itself" (*BP* §1). In other words, words developing the translation: the saying belongs to that which is to be said in that it somehow issues from it. That which is to be said is Being, for which from the outset Heidegger proposes various names—*Seyn* (with the archaic spelling), *das Wesen des Seyns, die Wahrheit des Seyns*—marking certain differences yet always, as he says, saying "the same of the same" (*BP* §39). He also says the same of the same when he writes—still almost at the beginning: "*Dieses Sagen sammelt das Seyn auf einen ersten Anklang seines Wesens und erklingt doch nur selbst aus diesem Wesen*" (*BP* §1). Here translation becomes hesitant and would like to surround virtually every decision with a discourse of strategy and reservation. The danger is, above all, that too much may already have been decided, if indecisively, when the passage is rendered in the following words: "This saying gathers Beyng into a first sounding of its essence and yet itself sounds only from out of this essence." To say it otherwise: this saying instigates a sounding or echoing and itself arises, sounds, from out of precisely that which it lets sound, that which it gathers into a sounding, namely, Beyng.

But what is required of such saying? How can one speak in a way that accords with crossing toward another beginning? In the first beginning, speech could remain in a sense the language *of beings,* for in the first beginning philosophy was addressed to beings in their Beingness (*Seiendheit*), that is, Being was thought only as the Beingness of beings, only from the perspective of beings. Now, however, the demand is to think Being, not from beings, as their Beingness, but from itself. Now speech cannot remain simply that of beings. Heidegger asks: "Can the truth of Beyng be directly said at all, if all language is indeed the language of beings? Or can a new language for Beyng be invented?" He answers both questions with a single word: "No." He adds: "And even if this should succeed and even without forming words artificially, this language would not be a language capable of saying" (*BP* §36). What is required, on the contrary, is that one take up, within certain limits, the ordinary words and, as Heidegger says, "go a certain stretch with them, in order then at the right moment to carry out a reversal but under the power of the same word" (*BP* §41). In other words, what is required is that one enact a kind of disjoining of language, that one throw the existing language out of joint, bringing it to say what otherwise it does not say, bringing it to say what, at the same time, one must come *to hear* precisely in the saying. This is why, as Heidegger insists in this context, "All saying must let the ability to hear arise with it."

Heidegger marks the difference between beginnings, between what they demand, *also* as a difference in thinking, as a difference *of* thinking. Referring to the first beginning, he writes: "'Thinking' in the ordinary and long since customary determination is the representation of something in its ἰδέα as the κοινόν, representation of something in general" (*BP* §27). Thus he indicates that thinking in the first beginning corresponds to the determination of the Being, that is, the Beingness, of beings as ἰδέα in the sense of κοινόν. In the first beginning, that is, with Plato and Aristotle, such thinking was—Heidegger grants—genuinely creative. Yet thinking in the other beginning is described by Heidegger in a very different way, both with respect to its moments and in its relation to man. Consider, for example, the following account; in it I deliberately leave the names of the moments—initially and except in a minimal way—untranslated, since these are among the most difficult to translate and in any case would, if translated, require a more extensive discourse than I can undertake here: "Inceptual thinking is the originary enactment [*Vollzug*] of *Anklang, Zuspiel, Sprung,* and *Gründung* in their unity. Enactment is intended here to say: that these—*Anklang, Zuspiel, Sprung, Gründung* in their unity—are humanly only taken over and sustained, that they themselves are always essentially something other and belong to the happening of Da-sein" (*BP* §27). At the very least one can say that to think inceptually—that is, crossing toward the other beginning—has nothing to do with representing things in their generality, in their whatness; such thinking is not a matter of representing, for instance, what man is, what god is, etc. Rather, it is a thinking that puts aside the classical Greek question τί ἐστι...? And doing so, it consists then in carrying out, enacting, the operations named in these words *Anklang, Zuspiel, Sprung, Gründung*; it consists—to venture only the merest translation—in hearing the sounding echo of Beyng so as to release a mutual passing between beginnings, enacting an abysmal leap to Beyng so as to let the truth of Beyng be grounded. And yet, these operations are not something that man simply does; they are not actions of a subject nor even simply operations of the being that each of us is. They are always essentially something other, and man only takes over and sustains in a certain way what properly belongs to the happening of Da-sein and thus to the happening of Beyng as such. Taking over these operations, man is in turn taken over and dislodged from being that which otherwise each of us himself is.

To come to belong to Being so as to speak from it is to undergo a displacement. To say Beyng as *Ereignis,* from *Ereignis,* is, in Heidegger's words, "*dem Er-eignis übereignet zu werden*" (*BP,* initial, unnumbered section). One could say—hardly pretending to translate—that it is a matter of being owned over to *Ereignis,* that is, again, displaced or—in another sense—translated. To be owned over to *Ereignis* amounts, says Heidegger, to "an essential transformation of man from rational animal into Da-sein." It is not just that the human is to be rethought as Da-sein rather than conceived as rational animal but rather that in the saying as such this transformation must be undergone. To come again to say Being in the wake of nihilism, in the very abandonment of Being, is to undergo a decisive transformation. It is to be displaced, to risk derangement.

Yet how, in the abandonment of Being, in the wake of withdrawal, is man drawn to Being? How does the human come to be owned over, appropriated, and thus displaced from being rational animal into being Da-sein? This displacement is possible, according to Heidegger, only if man is properly attuned—or comes to be so attuned—to Being in its very withdrawal. The fundamental attunement (*Grundstimmung*) required is complex, irreducible to a single mode such as wonder, which constituted the fundamental attunement in the first beginning. In the other beginning the attunement must be manifold, because it must open man to Being precisely through exposing him to beings bereft of Being. *Das Erschrecken, die Verhaltenheit, die Scheu*—these words, with the discourses gathered around them, name the moments of this attunement. This attunement not only opens the possibility of thoughtfully saying Being in the wake of nihilism but also sustains such saying throughout its course. In Heidegger's words: "All essential thinking requires that its thoughts and sentences be mined, like ore, every time anew out of the fundamental attunement. If the fundamental attunement is absent, then everything is a forced rattling of concepts and empty words" (*BP* §6).

Yet, granted that such thinking is sustained by the manifold attunement, what guise does it assume as such? In what form is this thoughtful saying of Beyng to be unfolded? Heidegger marks clearly its difference from metaphysical thinking. Metaphysical thinking proceeds from the inaugural determination of Being as Beingness (*Seiendheit*) and of Beingness as ἰδέα, hence, as purely anterior to the beings it determines. Thus metaphysical thinking assumes the form of regression from beings to their *a priori* condition. Heidegger observes: "Such a return has, therefore, become the basic form of 'metaphysical' thinking in manifold modifications, to such a degree that even the overcoming of 'metaphysics' toward an inceptual understanding cannot dispense with this way of thinking" (*BP* §44). And yet, even if thinking still must repeat up to a point the turn back to the *a priori*, it must, as it crosses to the other beginning, relinquish such regress and grant that Beyng is not an *a priori*, that, as Heidegger says, it "is not something 'earlier'—subsisting for and in itself" (*BP* §5).

Even aside from the differentiation of beginnings, Heidegger stresses the displacement that thinking undergoes. He observes that philosophy does not proceed by submitting propositions to proof. For all proof presupposes that the one who carries out the proof—proceeding from proposition to proposition—remains unchanged. "By contrast," Heidegger continues, "in philosophical knowing a transformation of the man who understands begins with the very first step. . . . The thinking of philosophy remains strange because in philosophical knowing everything comes at once to be displaced" (*BP* §5). Here one may recall the inaugural images: as one moves up the divided line, as one ascends from the cave, one not only comes to know ever more truly but also is oneself continually transformed. Plato designates this transformation by the word περιαγωγή, the turning around, the being turned around, of the soul. Once one has ascended from the cave and raised one's gaze to the heavens, one will have been so displaced that upon reentering the cave one will appear confused, even deranged.

In crossing to the other beginning, the transformation would be still more perilous. Heidegger signals this peril discreetly by the key word he uses twice in the passage (just cited) on the transformation undergone by the philosopher. He says that "*alles . . . in die Verrückung kommt*"; and he characterizes the specific transformation of the philosopher as "*Verrückung in das Da-sein selbst.*" The word means *displacement*, and yet it also suggests *verrückt* and *Verrücktheit, mad* and *madness.* The Platonic connection prompts the translation back into Greek, the translation μανία. This translation would become all the more compelling, were one to insist—as I would—on differentiating the thoughtful saying in the dialogues from the discourse of the first beginning.

The displacement that such manic saying undergoes is a displacement into Beyng. The genuine power of thinking consists in the capacity to undergo this displacement and to endure, as Heidegger says, "the strangeness of Beyng" (*BP* §18). This endurance requires also enduring the apparent powerlessness, that thinking brings about no immediate effect upon beings. Heidegger draws a connection with the solitude of the thinker (*die Einsamkeit des Denkers*). Such solitude, he insists, is a consequence of the genuine power of thinking. It is not as though one withdraws into solitude and therefore exercises no effect upon beings. Rather, because thinking requires that one turn away from beings and all effectings upon them to Beyng in its strangeness, in its apartness, one will always, in thinking, have withdrawn into solitude.

This displacement is not only a turn away from engagement with beings and with the effects otherwise brought about among them, but also—most remarkably—it is a displacement of the human being away from being a being as such. Here are Heidegger's words: "The less a being [*Je unseiender*] man is and the less he insists upon the being [*das Seiende*] that he finds himself to be, so much nearer does he come to Being [*Sein*]" (*BP* §83). The μανία of thinking, its manic saying, is such that the human being is displaced from itself as a being, is displaced from being the being that it itself is. Thinking requires the most radical loss of self, and it is in this madness that, properly attuned, one is drawn toward, opened to, the gift of Being.

Yet how does thinking unfold? Or, to risk—and at the same time also necessarily to displace—the classical question: What is philosophy? Though avoiding—deliberately no doubt—the classical form of the question, Heidegger nonetheless addresses it directly: "Philosophy: to find the simple looks and indigenous shapes and to bring them to appear so that the essency of Beyng is sheltered therein and taken to heart." He continues: "Who is capable of *both*: the farthest look into the concealed essence of Beyng and the nearest prospering of the shining shapes of sheltering beings" (*BP* §32). Philosophy seeks out certain looks and shapes. It seeks out the simple looks; and now, crossing to the other beginning, it seeks out looks that are neither apart from beings (as the εἴδη that constitute their Beingness) nor images of such pure, apart looks. Philosophy also seeks out indigenous shapes, shapes that belong to the region where humans are at home, shapes that shine forth there among the things that continue to surround humans even in their solitude, even when they are struck with madness. Philosophy brings these looks and shapes to appear, does so precisely through speech, indeed through the manic saying of Beyng. And yet, displaced into Beyng to such an extent as to have become even less itself a being, driven by its μανία away from beings and even from being a being, the philosopher finds these looks and shapes among beings and says them in such a way as to let Beyng be sheltered in them.

This is what philosophy will be. In Heidegger's words: "What remains for thinking is only the simplest saying of the simplest image in purest reticence. The future first thinker must be capable of this" (*BP* §32). Yet in the interest of such capability, that of thinking and speaking on the verge, the future thinker will not—let me add—be able to forgo the return to the beginning, which, in Heidegger's phrase, comes toward us from out of the future.

Index of Greek Words and Phrases

General Index of Words and Phrases

Hegel, Georg Wilhelm Friedrich, 9f.,
67 n. 13, 76
Heidegger, Martin, 3, 7f., 14f., 56;
Being and Time, 69–72, 140; *Contributions to Philosophy*, 14–23, 136–
48; *Einführung in die Metaphysik*,
64; "The End of Philosophy and
the Task of Thinking," 23; and
madness, 137, 139, 146–48; *Metaphysische Anfangsgründe der Logik*,
60; and nihilism, 136–41, 145; *Parmenides*, 27f.; *Plato's Doctrine of
Truth*, 17–23, 25; "The Question
Concerning Technology," 63;
and spirit, 63f.; *Unterwegs zur
Sprache*, 66; *Was heisst Denken?*,
60, 69; *Was Ist Metaphysik?*, 71;
"Das Wesen der Sprache," 66, 68–
70, 73; *Vom Wesen der Wahrheit*,
17 n. 3, 73; and *Wiederholung*,
56; *The Will to Power as Art*,
137
higher music. *See under* music
Hölderlin, 137
Homer, 116, 118

il y a, 102f.
intelligible/sensible, 3, 6, 14, 16, 44,
100, 136; and arithmetic, 49; inversion of, 14, 138; and metaphor, 104;
and *pharmakon*, 77, 94; and χώρα,
39, 77, 94, 97, 101

Krell, David Farrell, 60 n. 9, 61, 62 n.
11, 103 n. 33

l'autre nuit, 132, 137
last word, 53–56, 67
Laws, 105; and music, 117,
126–29
Lehre, 18. *See also* unsaid
Lichtung, 107

look of things, 19, 24. *See also* εἶδος;
see also ἰδέα

madness (*see* μανία), 91, 133, 135,
146; and ἔρως, 120f.; and excess,
120, 135; and *l'autre nuit*, 137; and
memory, 94, 100; and nihilism,
136f., 139; and solitude, 147f.
Mallet, Marie-Louise, 100f.
Martin, Henri, 32
memory, 92–94, 100
metaphor, 104, 140
music, 32, 39, 117–24; and the beautiful, 119–21; and dissolution into
lawlessness, 114f., 125–29; and
ἔρως, 119–21; in Greece, 116f.;
higher, 122–24; in the *Laws*, 117,
126–29; and madness, 120f., 133–35;
neglect of, 125f.; in the *Phaedo*, 123;
philosophical, 122–24; and politics,
110–16, 124–35; in the *Republic*, 113–
27, 130f.; and spirit, 112; strange,
114f.; in the *Timaeus*, 134f.; and
war, 124
myth (*see* μῦθος), 86–96; of Er, 130f.

Nietzsche, Friedrich Wilhelm, 7f., 16;
Gay Science, 136f.; and metaphor,
140; overturning of Platonism, 14,
137f.
nihilism, 136–41, 145
nocturnal day, 4f.

ones, 49f., 85, 93, 124
Orpheus, 78, 112, 129–35
other beginning, 7, 8, 10, 12–24, 95,
136, 142f., 145–48
other night, the. *See l'autre nuit*

Phaedo, 13, 33 n. 1, 45, 59, 123;
and blindness, 45, 51 n. 9;
and exorbitant Platonism, 108f.;